Sellers' Guide to Trademark Law

Table of Contents

Purpose of the Book:

We here at Rosenbaum Famularo, P.C., help e-commerce sellers around the world, who sell on a variety of online platforms, protect their intellectual property rights and overall brand. This book focuses on informing our sellers about protecting their brand and the steps that can be taken to prohibit infringers. We will discuss both trademark and copyright law, the two primary ways to protect your brand.

There are two main goals of this book:

- Educate online sellers about trademark law and how it affects them.
- Teach online sellers how to protect their trademarks from infringement or avoid infringing on others.

Firm Profile:

Rosenbaum Famularo, P.C., focuses on the needs of Online Sellers. We have lawyers, paralegals, former online sellers, and others on staff around the world. Our clients have the opportunity to meet with us, in person, at locations in New York, Shenzhen, Yiwu and Melbourne.

Online Sellers are not alone anymore.

Rosenbaum Famularo, P.C., the law firm behind AmazonSellersLawyer.com has obtained the reinstatement of countless Amazon Sellers' accounts and listings. The firm has obtained retractions of complaints from numerous brands and resolved many issues with Amazon's staff in the United States, India, Ireland, Costa Rica, and the United Kingdom.

The partners of the firm, CJ Rosenbaum and Anthony Famularo regularly speak at events for Sellers around the world.

Rosenbaum Famularo's other books include:

- *Amazon Law Library, Volume 1*
- *Your Guide to Amazon Suspensions*
- *Your Guide to Selling Fashion on Amazon*
- *Amazon Sellers' Guide to Copyright Law, and*
- *Amazon Sellers' Guide to Trademark Law*

Rosenbaum Famularo provides more free content for Amazon Sellers than any other company or law firm. If you want to learn more about Intellectual Property law for e-commerce Sellers, please visit one of our following social media accounts:

- Instagram: @RosenbaumFamularo
- ASL Twitter: @AmazonSellerLaw
- RF Twitter: @Merchprotection

- YouTube Channel: Rosenbaum Famularo, P.C.
- Facebook: Amazon Sellers' Lawyer
- Websites: amazonsellerslawyer.com and rosenbaumfamularo.com
- Google Plus: Rosenbaum Famularo
- LinkedIn: Rosenbaum Famularo
- Reddit: Amazon Sellers Lawyer (u/Rosenbaum Famularo)

Since starting my practice in 1994, I have represented entrepreneurs who operate both online and brick & mortar businesses. I am also a courtroom lawyer and litigator. I have represented people across the United States, have taken countless depositions, and tried more cases each year than most lawyers do during their entire careers.

I have successfully litigated cases against some of the largest corporations in the world, including: McDonald's, Sears, Kentucky Fried Chicken, and many insurance companies.

- In NYC, I have successfully obtained redress for my clients against the NYPD, the NYC Housing Department, the NYC Health and Hospitals Corp., and other behemoths.
- I have represented clients in the internet, finance, health and entertainment industries.
- I have been admitted to practice law in state and federal courts.

- I hold executive and leadership roles in the NYS Bar Association and the National American Association for Justice.
- I have delivered lectures to other lawyers in New York, Chicago, Montreal, Maryland, Florida and California.

Authors

CJ Rosenbaum, Esq.

CJ is the founder of the firm. He is known around the world for teaching tens of thousands of Amazon Sellers how to avoid suspensions. CJ teaches Amazon Sellers how to get their accounts back efficiently is they suffer a suspension of their Amazon Sellers' Account or the loss of the ability to sell one or more specific products. CJ has published thousands of pages of free guidance for Amazon Sellers. CJ started focusing on helping Amazon Sellers years ago after learning that Amazon Sellers needed someone that could analyze accounts, draft concise and persuasive Plans of Action, address intellectual property issues and also represent Amazon Sellers against Amazon at arbitrations when Amazon refuses to amicably resolve issues. CJ uses his extensive prior education and experience in business and business law, negotiations, law for entrepreneurs and his fifteen years as a trial lawyer to help Amazon Sellers.

Prior to CJ, there was seemingly nobody who understood what was needed to win an arbitration and was then able to use that information to analyze accounts and draft persuasive Plans of Action. Fast forward to today, CJ, and his partner, Anthony Famularo, are responsible for saving thousands of Amazon Sellers' Accounts, thousands of businesses and likely tens of thousands of jobs around the world.

As Amazon Sellers pivoted into developing their own Private Label Brands, CJ, Anthony and the entire team at Rosenbaum Famularo, P.C., grew to help Private Label Sellers. The number one firm for helping Amazon Sellers is also the number one firm to help Sellers as they develop, monitor and protect their brands and their intellectual property rights.

Having written the books on selling on Amazon, CJ, Anthony and their firm law are uniquely qualified to help Sellers protect their intellectual property rights.

Anthony Famularo

Anthony is the Managing Partner at Rosenbaum Famularo, P.C. Anthony has worked with CJ from the beginning of the focus on Amazon Sellers. Anthony's experience includes addressing tens of thousands of issues related to Amazon and other e-commerce Sellers and intellectual property issues.

After working with CJ and saving countless accounts and jobs across the United States as the New York Managing Attorney, Anthony was made a Partner of the firm in 2016.

Anthony manages a team of over twenty lawyers, paralegals and support staff around the world.

Anthony has written or edited more Plans of Action than anyone in the world.

Authors:

Christopher Abiuso

I am a 2019 J.D. Candidate at the Maurice A. Deane School of Law at Hofstra University. After graduating from Stony Brook University in 2014 with a degree in psychology, I pursued a legal education to further align my interests with my career. I am a Notes Editor for the *Hofstra Law Review* and was one of four people to construct and grade Hofstra Law's writing competition, which nearly all first-year law students participate. Furthermore, I am following the Intellectual Property Law Honors Concentration and a member of the Hofstra Intellectual Property Law Association. As an Eagle Scout, I am no stranger to the rigors of hard work and dedication.

Benjamin Lobley

I am a 2020 Juris Doctor candidate currently attending the Maurice A. Deane School of Law at Hofstra University. I hold a Bachelor of Arts in Political Science and History from the University of Vermont. In addition to my work with Rosenbaum Famularo, P.C., I will be serving as the Treasurer for the Veterans Law Student Association and have been selected to the Junior Staff for Volume 44 of the American College of Trust and Estate Counsel Law Journal at Hofstra University. Once I graduate from law school, I intend to practice Intellectual Property law. When I am not studying or working, I enjoy playing tennis, sailing and reading good books.

Editor

Adina Grodsky

I am 2021 Juris Doctor Candidate at the New England School of Law. I hold a Bachelor of Arts degree in Political Science, and a minor in Chinese language.

Illustrator

Dave Kopka

Brooklyn-based artist and graphic designer. Illustrator for the entire *Sellers' Guide to* series with Rosenbaum Famularo, P.C.

- Email: illustration@davekopka.com.
- Website: davekopka.com.

CHAPTER 1: WHEN SHOULD A TRADEMARK BE PURSUED, AND WHEN IS IT BEST TO WALK AWAY?

I.   What Is a Trademark?

Keurig. Starbucks. Barilla. McDonalds. Tide.

These five trademarks (all of them are word marks) all bestow certainty upon the goods and services associated with them–certainty in quality, standards, uses, and, indeed, even what *types* of goods and services may be generally expected.

- Keurig's machines are compatible with K-cups;

- Starbucks is associated with fast and dependable service and particular, rather strong, coffee;

- Barilla sells respectable Italian pastas and sauces at a reasonable price;

- McDonalds has specific tasting burgers and fries;

- Tide will never be expected to move into producing food items.

It is important to note that these certainties do not apply directly to the goods or the services provided. While one can assume that a burger from McDonalds will take about a minute to make and will taste just about the same as the last, this is primarily because of *where* the burger is coming from and the standard of consistent quality which has been associated with its point of origin.

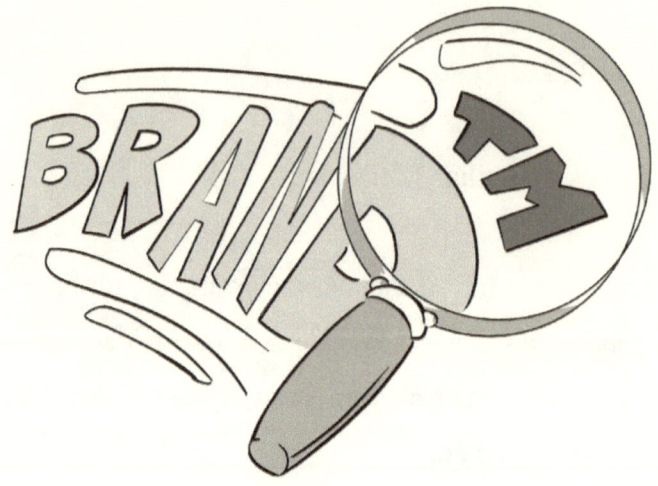

Trademarks are an old and established tradition in the realm of merchants and commerce. In fact, the earliest "trademarks" date back to 5000 B.C. in China, where pottery was stamped with the location of its creation and its manufacturer.[1]

In ancient Egypt, craftsmen affixed unique symbols to their goods so buyers would be able to easily determine the product's origin.[2]

Over time, this tradition of marking goods with the symbol or signature of their point of origin expanded to encompass all of Europe,

---

[1] *History of Trademarks: Everything You Need to Know*, UPCOUNSEL (last visited July 20, 2018), https://www.upcounsel.com/history-of-trademarks.
[2] *Id.*

growing particularly prominent in the middle ages.[3] King Edward I of England, in the 12th century, enacted a law which made it illegal for a jeweler to sell a piece of jewelry lacking the stamp of the royal office known as the Goldsmith's Hall. The punishment for counterfeiting this mark was death.[4]

Although these early proto-trademarks were not the fully-fledged trademarks of today, they fulfilled the function of preventing fraudulent products from being developed and distributed.

The modern trademark saw its first use in its earliest form in the time between the 13th and 16th centuries as the merchant mark.[5] Trade guilds used specific marks to indicate the origin of their goods, first by bell makers and then by paper makers.[6]

Southern v. How, an English case from 1618, is generally regarded as the earliest known court case involving trademark infringement, which came about when a low-tier clothmaker used a mark which was legally reserved for high-tier clothmakers.[7]

---

[3] *Id.*
[4] *Id.*
[5] *Id.*
[6] *Id.*
[7] David Johnson, *Trademarks: A History*, INFOPLEASE (last visited July 20, 2018), https://www.infoplease.com/trademarks-history.

Trademarks have grown so prevalent that they have seemingly come to define not just the manufacturers of goods, but products themselves. Instead of relying on what judges rule on from case to case, merchants depend on the Lanham Act, which was signed into law 1946, to offer legal armor against infringing parties, by introducing a series of laws meant to protect the sanctity of trademarks.[8] Grocery store shelves, magazines, and television advertisements are filled to the brim with an endless stream of trademarks used by sellers to promote and sell their particular brand of product. Mentally, it has become very easy for what began as an indication of product origin to become a label for the product itself.

Thinking that a trademark defines the product is a mistake. Trademarks do not describe the goods in question. If that were the case, Apple products purchasers would be disappointed, indeed, to see a phone or laptop in their packages and not pieces of fruit. A more accurate explanation is that trademarks identify the *origin* of goods to consumers; in other words, they identify the *Seller*. All of his or her good nature, dependability, the overall quality of the goods he or she

---

[8] Beverly W. Pattishall, *The Lanham Trademark Act at Fifty – Some History and Comment*, 86 TRADEMARK REP. 442, 442 (1996). The Lanham Act was written to simplify the trademark process. Although not imperative to know, it may interest sellers to know that when they are able to safely register their trademarks against infringement and are able to bring a lawsuit against infringers, they have the Lanham Act to thank. *Id.* at 442-43. As one of the most important sources of law for trademarks, this book will return at frequent intervals to reference this Act. While it is not necessary to follow closely along, sellers may wish to keep some of the more important sections handy to discourage infringing parties from continuing use of their offending trademark.

produces, and even his or her public image can be directly applied to the trademark. Any product bearing this trademark, in effect, affirms to consumers that they are guaranteed the same generalized standards of quality and care that have been demonstrated in the past by goods advertised by or labeled with such a trademark. It grants to consumers a sense of security in that the product they are purchasing will not stray too far from what they have thus far expected.

Although trademarks may seem dedicated to consumer protection, they are also fundamental to establishing the Seller's territory of business, from geographic location, to product category, to the particular type of product, to the assurances the Seller can typically guarantee to consumers. An effective trademark is a means of identifying and separating the Seller's goods from those of competitors, or even those who are not directly competitors but with whom association would injure the Seller's image. Imagine, for example, the effect on the public opinion of the dog food company Alpo if another company specializing in rat poison was able to brand their products with the "ALPO" logo. Besides the obvious and distressing consequences which would befall consumers who become confused by such labeling, Alpo would also have a huge problem; they would seemingly be associated with a brand of rat poison. They would have to contend with an endless stream of questions as consumers, some of whom having potentially bought Alpo dog food before, ask them, "Are you selling rat poison now? Is there a risk of contamination with the dog food? Will your quality slip now that you are focusing on both dog food *and* rat poison?" Even if Alpo fielded and answered every single question with the answer that they are not associated with "ALPO," "ALPO" will continue to sell rat poison while Alpo continues to deal with an intense identity crisis in trying to reach and educate other newly-confused consumers that Alpo is *not* "ALPO" and is not even associated with "ALPO." If that last sentence confused or frustrated you, consider yourself in the shoes of a similarly confused or frustrated consumer. This is the confusion and frustration which a trademark will work to prevent.

Justice Pitney once said that trademarks "designate . . . goods as the product of a particular [seller] and . . . protect his [or her] good will against the sale of another's product as his [or hers]."[9] As such, trademarks are a form of protection for not only consumers but also sellers. Without them, a Seller's goods could easily be attributed to another individual selling similar goods. This false Seller may hijack the sweat of the Seller's brow and abuse the good nature he or she has worked to foster. This false Seller may sell inferior goods which are then mistakenly attributed to the legitimate Seller, injuring his or her reputation. Designing and using a trademark to designate a seller's goods as coming from that Seller and that Seller alone may therefore appear to be good idea. However, before being drafted and used, a trademark must be the first of its kind to be used; in other words, it must

---

[9] United Drug Co. v. Theodore Rectanus Co., 248 U.S. 90, 97 (1918).

have priority. What's more, it must satisfy a number of other legal requirements before its full protective power can be enjoyed.

II. Geographic Zones: When to Commit to a Trademark and When to Take a Step Back

A trademark would be worthless if any newcomer could register a mark that is similar to a mark that already exists. When a seller is deciding on a trademark to use, therefore, it is important to ensure that another existing trademark does not have priority. That is to say, the Seller's prospective trademark must be the first in commercial use within its geographic area.

Typically, a trademark which is unregistered with the United States Patent and Trademark Office ("USPTO") will be limited to a general geographic area where the consumer base will be able to identify the mark as representing a particular source. This geographic area is called the "zone of goodwill."[10] A seller's zone of goodwill is comprised of both the zone of market penetration (regions where consumers have purchased products bearing the mark) and the zone of reputation (regions where consumers know about the seller's products).[11] Further, to gain trademark protection in the zone of goodwill, a Seller must demonstrate that their mark has been used in

---

[10] W. Scott Creasman, *Establishing Geographic Rights in Trademarks Based on Internet Use*, 95 TRADEMARK REP. 1016, 1017 (2005).
[11] *Id.* at 1017-18.

commerce by showing the volume of sales in the area, the growth trends in that area, the number of customers in relation to the number of actual customers in the area, and the advertising present within the area.[12] A trademark that satisfies these requirements and is the first of its kind to

be used in the zone of goodwill, will have legal priority over any newcomers who will be infringing on the senior patent if they decide to enter the market without priority.

Much like brick-and-mortar merchants, internet sellers who are attempting to form and use a trademark will need to worry about another trademark holding priority over theirs in the desired geographic area. Like Sellers who sell a majority of their merchandise in physical locations, internet sellers must keep in mind the market penetration and reputation of competitors and their potentially prioritized trademarks to

---

[12] *Id.* at 1018.

determine what areas may be off limits for to their own trademark.[13] Market penetration for an internet seller may be easily determined by looking at the number and distribution of total sales made by the internet Seller. Although imperfect, reputation can at least be estimated by reviewing the number of views from each geographic location the Seller would like to deploy the trademark in.

> CJ's Tip: When you're creating a trademark for your brand, it's always good practice to know when to put it into use and when to walk away. You shouldn't spend too much time or effort on designing and employing a particular trademark if you know it will probably be blocked by a preexisting mark. If, after checking the area or the Gazette (discussed in later chapters), and you think it would be impossible to avoid infringing on another's mark, it's always easier to take a step back and redesign your mark than to cast the die and hope your trademark won't step on any toes. If you don't take the time to check the Gazette or the area you want to deploy your trademark in for a preexisting mark, you will probably be surprised when you receive a cease and desist order, or even worse, a legal complaint.

---

[13] *Id.* at 1029-30.

Reviewing the zone of goodwill of competitors before filing a trademark to avoid infringement should, of course, always be done. However, if the Seller, for whatever reason, has no plans to pursue registration of his or her trademark, it may be beneficial to perform regular checks of his or her own zone of goodwill to measure the geographic area his or her trademark covers. In this way, not only will the internet Seller avoid infringing any existing trademarks, but he or she will also be able to more readily determine his or her zone of goodwill for the purposes of protecting his or her own territory. This book will go deeper into watching and protecting a trademark from infringement in chapter 8.[14]

In addition to the above, also of importance in determining the geographic zone in which to deploy one's trademark, is the predicted zone of expansion for the business. This zone of expansion can be determined by first looking at whether the owner of the mark holds a valid trademark. Next an observer should evaluate: the physical distance from the trademark user's location to the perimeter of the claimed zone; the business and size of the market; the history of expansion and estimation of when the user could reach the zone in question; and whether the expansion into the zone would be the next probable step for the business's expansion.[15] Because of the widespread nature of the internet, it has been noted that the zone of expansion for internet sellers

---

[14] *See infra* Chapter 8.
[15] Michelle L. Evans, 99 AM. JUR. PROOF OF FACTS 3d 107 *Establishing the Zone of Expansion for Trademark Purposes* § 18 (2018).

may in fact be larger and quicker to grow. This is because the internet is available to so many people at once and it would be easier to assume that the internet seller will be able to expand to a larger number of people than a brick-and-mortar store.[16]

> Anthony's Breakdown: When dealing with trademark priority issues, you may come across the concept of tacking. Tacking is where a party "tacks" or "saves" the date of the original mark onto a subsequent mark for purposes of establishing priority. However, the two marks must be so similar that consumers would typically regard them as the same. For example, if McDonald's started a subsequent business under the mark "McRonald's" as a cardiologist office to fix the hearts of people who eat too many Big Mac's, they would be able to tack the new mark to the date they registered "McDonald's" for trademark. This is because the marks are so similar that any average person would recognize the subsequent mark as part of McDonald's business. This is a fairly advanced and rare concept to deal with, but it may come in handy to know if you ever want to draft a new trademark and don't want to start fresh with its priority.

---

[16] *See* Brian L. Berlandi, *What State am I in?: Common Law Trademarks on the Internet*, 4 MICH. TELECOMM. & TECH. L. REV. 105, 113-21 (1999).

The theory and practice of establishing and maintaining a trademark may seem daunting at first, but it is important to keep abreast of it to maintain a solid brand. The chapters that follow will make both the theory and practice of trademarks, as applied to internet sellers, much easier to comprehend.

CHAPTER 2: THE REGISTRATION PROCESS

I.   Introduction

The application for federal registration of a trademark with the USPTO is fairly simple. The process is primarily based on the federal statutes and regulations on trademarks.

CJ's Side Note: It is **crucial** to register your trademark to protect your product from being infringed upon. Without registering the trademark, your ability to enforce your intellectual property rights is limited to your geographic area. In contrast, if you register with the USPTO, your trademark will be extended to the entirety of the US.

There are three methods Sellers can base their trademark application on:

(1) actual use of the mark in commerce;

(2) actual intent to use the mark in commerce; or

(3) a foreign application for registration, or a foreign registration, of the mark.[17]

---

[17] JAMES E. HAWES & AMANDA V. DWIGHT, 1 TRADEMARK REGISTRATION PRAC. § 3:1 (2018 ed.).

There are separate applications with different principles for each ground.[18] Due to the similarity of the registration processes, it can be assumed that, unless otherwise specified, the text of this chapter discusses the registration process when the trademark has already been in commercial use.

II.   Specimen and Declaration of Use

Whether the Seller is applying to register a trademark already in use or a trademark which will eventually be put into use, the "specimen" will be submitted at the very beginning of the registration process. The specimen is a drawing or representation of the mark which the Seller wishes to register. Ultimately, this specimen should:

(1)   accurately display the mark;

(2)   show the association between the mark and the goods; and

(3)   describe how the mark will be used in commerce.[19] The following graph may help in determining what would be acceptable forms of specimens:

---

[18] *Id.*
[19] *Id.*

eptable Specimens	Unacceptable Specimens
ags or labels affixed to the ds of the container for the ds. tampings on the goods or a container. astruction sheets packaged a the goods. creen captures showing the ck displayed with the ds.	• Advertising • Invoices • Price-lists • Business letterhead

There are several points in the registration process where Sellers must file a document which swears that he or she is actually using the trademark in commerce. This document is called an affidavit or declaration of use or continued use. Failure to provide the declaration will either result in a rejection of the registration at the onset of the process or, in the case of the declaration of continued use, cancellation of the Seller's registered trademark.[20]

---

[20] *Id.* § 3:27; BREND A. OLSON, 20B2 MINN. PRAC., BUS. REG. IN MINNESOTA – FEDERAL § 2.160 (2018 ed.).

This section of the chapter will deal with the declaration of use, which occurs after the mark has been used in commerce but before the mark has been registered. For information regarding the affidavit of continued use, which is submitted after the registration has been granted at frequent intervals, please read ahead to Section IV of this chapter.

The declaration of use is one of the first documents to be submitted in the registration process to the USPTO. In the declaration, the applicant will be asserting and confirming that: (1) he or she is the owner of the trademark to be registered; (2) the mark is actually being used in the field of commerce specified in the application; (3) no other individual or business has the right to use the particular mark in commerce; (4) the specimens (discussed later) which are submitted with the declaration are accurate in how they portray the mark being used with the product; (5) the facts in the application are accurate and truthful; and (6) all statements made in the application are, to the applicant's knowledge, truthful.[21] These declarations do not require applicant Sellers to investigate or research whether another has a conflicting trademark, nor does it require knowledge if the mark in question is registered in another country. These are not grounds for disqualifying the application since the boundary of being registered with the USPTO is the U.S. border.[22] However, any prior knowledge held while making this declaration of another Seller having rights to a

---

[21] *See* HAWES & DWIGHT, *supra* note 17 § 3:27.
[22] *Id.*

sufficiently similar mark may be considered to be fraud against the USPTO, which would be considered a federal crime.[23]

> Anthony's Advice: Although the words "federal crime" might be scary, they are more of a deterrent against possible trademark infringers. As long as you present yourself honestly and to the best of your ability, you will be fine since it is not your responsibility to go out of your way to research others with potentially similar marks. Besides, since you will most likely be submitting your declaration through and with the aid of an experienced intellectual property law firm, you will have more than enough help in correctly submitting your declaration of use.

III.   Examination

Once the declaration and specimen have been submitted to the USPTO, the application will be examined by an "examiner." An examiner is an attorney employed by the USPTO. It usually takes about three months for an examiner to assigned to an application.[24] The examiner will review the trademark application for accuracy and applicability.[25]   During examination, the examiner will review the

---

[23] *Id.*
[24] *Second Quarter FY 2018, At a Glance*, USPTO (last visited July 16, 2018), https://www.uspto.gov/dashboards/trademarks/main.dashxml; Arthur L. Plevy, *How to Obtain Patents, Trademarks and Copyrights*, 161-JUN N.J. LAW. 12, 44 (1994).
[25] Plevy, *supra* note 24, at 44.

Official Gazette ("Gazette"), a collection of registered trademarks, to determine if there is a confusingly similar mark already registered with the USPTO.[26] If such a confusion-inducing similar mark is discovered, the examiner will contest or outright reject the application.[27]

There are other reasons for which the examiner may reject or contest the application, such as a lack of distinctiveness; this is an issue which will be discussed more in depth later in this book. Further, while the Gazette is also discussed later in this book, all that must be understood for now is that the Gazette is a collection of all trademarks registered with the USPTO.[28]

---

[26] *Id.*
[27] *Id.*
[28] *Id.*

If the examiner determines that there are contestable aspects of the trademark application, he or she may initiate an "office action" to block registration.[29] An office action is a preliminary rejection of the application. Office actions are directed at whatever the examiner deems most offending, whether it is a preexisting mark in the Gazette or a lack of distinctiveness.[30] During this contention, the examiner will support his or her claim about the mark's lack of registrability similar to any normal court action. The applicant will have six months to respond to the office action.[31] Legal counsel is highly recommended in this period of time to support the Seller's mark against the contentions raised by the examiner.

If the examiner finds no issues with the trademark application, or the Seller defeats the office action, the examiner will place the mark into the Gazette.[32] After this publication, there follows a period of 30 days, during which third parties who believe they will be injured by the publication may file an opposition.[33] Assuming there is no opposition, or the applicant is able to defeat any opposition which is filed, the registration will be official.

---

[29] *Id.* at 15.
[30] *Id.* at 15, 44.
[31] *Trademarks – What Happens Next?*, USPTO (last visited July 16, 2018), https://www.uspto.gov/trademarks-getting-started/trademark-basics/trademarks-what-happens-next.
[32] Plevy, *supra* note 24, at 44.
[33] USPTO, *supra* note 31.

IV.   Continued Use

After a trademark has been successfully registered with the USPTO, the Seller must file an affidavit claiming the continued use of the mark five years after registration.[34] After, a declaration of continued use must be submitted at every 10-year anniversary of the registration.[35] Failing to submit such declarations in a timely matter may lead to the cancelation of the trademark.[36]

The declaration must include a certified statement providing evidence of use in commerce or excusable nonuse of the trademark within the period designated in the Act.[37] It must also include:

(1) the U.S. registration number;

(2) the fee required for each class that the declaration covers;

(3) the grade period surcharge per class; and

(4) if a fee is submitted for a multiple-class registration, it must cover all the classes.[38]

If it does not cover all the classes and does not specify which class the fee should cover, the USPTO will issue a notice requiring

---

[34] *How Long Does Trademark Protection Last*, REGISTERINGATRADEMARK.COM (last visited July 16, 2018), http://www.registeringatrademark.com/length-trademark.shtml.
[35] *Id.*
[36] *See* OLSEN, note 4 § 2.160.
[37] *Id.*
[38] *Id.*

either a submission of the additional fees or to clarify to which class the fee should be applied.[39]

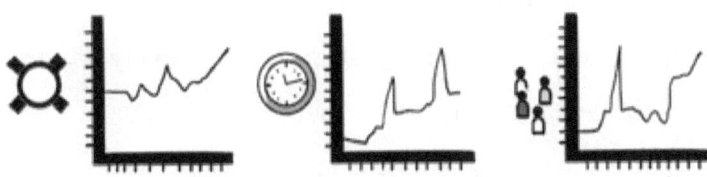

       The declaration must specify the nature of the goods or services that the trademark is for and how they are used in commerce. If it is not in use, the declaration must state when the use in commerce stopped and when the use is expected to resume.[40] Furthermore, it must assert the special circumstances that excuse the nonuse and state that the trademark was not abandoned.[41] Missing the date to file the declaration of continued use can have the potentially disastrous consequence of having your trademark registration cancelled; so, it should certainly never be overlooked.

V.   Intent to Use

       When the mark has not yet been used in commerce, a seller can apply for the mark to be filed if they have a genuine intent to use the mark in commerce.

---

[39] *Id.*
[40] *Id.*
[41] *Id.*

CJ's Side Note: The Lanham Act defines commerce as "all commerce that can be regulated by Congress." In other words, your mark must be used in interstate commerce. If you only plan to conduct business solely on a statewide level, it may not amount to a genuine intent to participate in interstate commerce and will prohibit you from getting your trademark federally registered.

Sellers who file an intent to use ("ITU") do not necessarily need to have their trademark to be in use before beginning the registration process.[42] Instead, the Seller must show that their mark has entered commerce at one of three points in the registration process: (1) before the application has been approved by the examiner; (2) within six months of filing the ITU; and (3) within one of the three six-month extensions available to the applicant.[43]

With an ITU application, Sellers gain priority rights in a trademark, but only if they actually use the mark in commerce at a later date.[44] Once an ITU application is filed, any subsequent users of the trademark will be given constructive notice of the contingent

---

[42] *Trademark Applications – Intent-to-Use (ITU) Basis*, USPTO (last visited July 16, 2018), https://www.uspto.gov/trademarks-application-process/filing-online/intent-use-itu-applications.
[43] *Id.*
[44] *Id.*

trademark.[45] The Seller who has filed an ITU application has priority of rights to the mark, even if the junior user begins using the mark first.[46] In other words, the priority date will relate back to the initial day that the Seller submitted the ITU application, not the day on which the Seller finally uses the trademark in commerce. In order to complete the registration process, Sellera must file an amendment to allege use or a statement of use after being given a notice of allowance.[47]

> CJ's Tip: Since the priority date of an ITU relates back to the date you file the ITU, instead of when you actually put the mark into commercial use, it is the best decision to file an ITU immediately after you decide to design and utilize a trademark. Any applicant who tries to register a similar mark in the time you develop the mark will be blocked from fully registering, unless you fail to actually put the mark into use within the allotted time.

VI.   Madrid System

The international protection of trademarks is based on the Madrid System, which is governed by the World Intellectual Property Organization ("WIPO") and is comprised of 117 member nations. There are two registration systems within the Madrid System: (1) the

---

[45] *Id.*
[46] *Id.*
[47] *Id.*

Madrid Agreement and (2) the Madrid Protocol.[48] The United States is a signatory only of the Madrid Protocol, meaning U.S. sellers can only register their trademark under the rules of the Madrid Protocol if registering abroad.[49] After obtaining a basic mark, an applicant may then file a Form MM2 international application through the Madrid System via his or her Office of origin.[50] If an international application designates the United States, the applicant must then file Form MM18.[51] The applicant's Office of origin will then file Form MM2 and, if applicable, Form MM18 on behalf of the applicant with WIPO, who will examine the application, register the mark in the International Register, and publish the mark in the Gazette of International Marks.[52] The examination may take 12 to 18 months, after which the scope of protection will be determined.[53] The outcome of registering through the Madrid Protocol is that the Seller's mark will be registered in the foreign country which registration is desired in.[54] If this seems confusing, sellers need not worry; an experienced intellectual property firm is more than apt to file through the Madrid Protocol. The bullets below may also help to break down the pros and cons of registering through the Madrid Protocol.

---

[48] *See generally, Madrid – The International Trademark System*, WIPO (last visited July 16, 2018), http://www.wipo.int/madrid/en.
[49] *Id.*
[50] *Id.*
[51] *Id.*
[52] *Id.*
[53] *Id.*
[54] *Id.*

Advantages:

- Allows sellers to submit a single application and designate the protected countries.

- Works to the full extent of an application filed in any single country that is a part of the Madrid System.

- If the trademark office of a designated country doesn't deny the application within a specific period, the mark will be protected as if it has been accepted by the home office.

- Simplifies maintenance → possible to make subsequent changes and simple to renew.

Disadvantages:

- Scope of the trademark will be identical to scope of underlying U.S. trademark.

- U.S. specification is narrowly tailored because it requires proof of use before registration can be issued.

- National filings outside the U.S. not done through the Madrid System → not limited by U.S. specification and can be broadened so the seller enjoys the broadest possible protection.

- If the home country application fails for any reason → the application in any of the designated countries will fail as well.

Additionally, because there are significant differences in the fees and costs associated with filing through the Madrid System depending on the countries selected, the chart on the following page has been provided to help break down what the Seller may be expected to pay in a few select countries at the time of this book's publication. It must be remembered that there are many more countries involved than are listed and that these prices could change at any time. For the full and possibly updated list, please visit the WIPO website directly.[55]

Countries	Initial Fees	Renewal
Australia	263F* ($265.74) for each class of goods or services	300F ($303.12) for each class of goods or services
China	249F ($251.59) for one class 125F ($126.30) for each additional class *Where the mark is a collective mark:* 747F ($754.78) for one class 374F ($377.89) for each additional class	498F ($503.19) for one class 249F ($251.59) for each additional class

---

[55] *Individual Fees Under the Madrid Protocol*, WIPO (last updated June 2, 2018), http://www.wipo.int/madrid/en/fees/ind_taxes.html.

European Union	897F ($906.34) for the first class of goods or services	897F ($906.34) for the first class of goods or services
	55F ($55.57) for the second class	55F ($55.57) for the second class
	164F ($165.71) for each additional class	164F ($165.71) for each additional class
	Where the mark is a collective or certification mark:	*Where the mark is a collective or certification mark:*
	1531F ($1546.94) for the first class of goods or services	1531F ($1546.94) for the first class of goods or services
	55F ($55.57) for the second class	55F ($55.57) for the second class
	164F ($165.71) for each additional class	164F ($165.71) for each additional class
Mexico	149F ($150.55) for each class of goods or services	160F ($161.67) for each class of goods or services
United Kingdom	227F ($229.36) for one class	252F ($254.62) for one class
	63F ($63.66) for each additional class	63F ($63.66) for each additional class
United States of America	388F ($392.04) for each class of goods or services	291F ($294.03) for each class of goods or services

*F = Swiss Franc

CHAPTER 3: DESIGNING A REGISTRABLE TRADEMARK

I. Introduction

Under the Lanham Act, a trademark is defined as "any word, name, symbol, or device, or any combination thereof" which is used to indicate the origin or producer of specific goods.[56] Trademarks are not relegated to mere sight alone, however. Trademarks that are comprised of sounds (sound marks) are very common and have a history of garnering protection from both the courts and the USPTO through caselaw and registration.[57] Trademarks which rely on a specific color may, on some occasions, be held as valid as well, although with less uniformity or reliability.[58] Even scents have been considered a trademark, albeit in an even smaller number of circumstances and with even less uniformity in decisions.[59] In certain cases, the actual look, or "trade dress," of the product itself may be considered a variant of a trademark. Trade Dress is discussed in chapter 4.

---

[56] 15 U.S.C. § 1127 (2016).

[57] *See, e.g., In re* General Electric Broadcasting Company, Inc., 199 U.S.P.Q. 560 (T.T.A.B. 1978); *Trademark: "Sound Mark" Examples*, USPTO (last visited June 16, 2018), https://www.uspto.gov/trademark/soundmarks/trademark-sound-mark-examples (hosting a collection of sound marks which are either registered or pending registration (quoting Qualitex Co. v. Jacobson Products Co., Inc., 514 U.S. 159, 161 (1995) (holding that occasionally "a color will meet ordinary legal trademark requirements")).

[58] *See* Daniel Zendel & Dennis Prahl, *Making Sense of Trademarks: Colors, Sounds, & Scents*, LADAS & PARRY (Feb. 16, 1996), https://ladas.com/education-center/making-sense-trademarks-colors-sounds-scents.

[59] *See* Zendel & Prahl, *supra* note 58 (citing *In re* Clarke, 17 U.S.P.Q.2d 1238 (T.T.A.B. 1990) (holding that a floral scent could be considered a trademark when applied to sewing thread)).

As already discussed, for a trademark to be officially registered with the USPTO, the trademark must be distinctive. This applies to all trademark variants, from words to symbols to sound to trade dress. If the USPTO does not find the trademark to be distinctive of the source, it should be rejected by the examiner. Without distinctiveness, therefore, a mark is just a mark, a word is just a word, and a sound is just a sound, without any of the legal protections of a trademark.

Although it could seem a simple task to create a distinctive trademark, oftentimes the goals of making a distinctive trademark and memorable for the sake of consumer attraction and retention are at odds with each other. Without distinctiveness, however, there is no trademark. A careful balance, therefore, must be struck between distinctiveness and sensible designs and choices meant to interface with consumers and customers.

II.   Distinctiveness

When a trademark is "distinctive," it is a reference to how the trademark relates to the brand not the product itself.[60] In other words, a distinctive trademark is a mark which does not refer to the product itself. The mark refers back to the brand or manufacturer.

The accepted variations of distinctive marks are those which are suggestive, arbitrary, or fanciful.[61]

---

[60] Two Pesos, Inc. v. Taco Cabana, 505 U.S. 763, 769 (1992).
[61] Abercrombie & Fitch Co. v. Hunting World, Inc., 537 F.2d 4, 9 (1976).

Opposite to distinctive trademarks are trademarks which describe the product itself, of which the two variations are descriptive

and generic marks.[62]

Placed in order of least protectible to most protectible, the scale of distinctiveness is as follows:

(1) Generic

(2) Descriptive

(3) Suggestive

(4) arbitrary, and

(5) fanciful.[63]

---

[62] *Id.*

[63] *Id. See also*, U.S. PAT. AND TRADEMARK OFF., TRADEMARK MANUAL OF EXAMINING PROCEDURE (TMEP) § 1209.01 (2017).

There is no concrete rule to determine what marks are specifically generic or suggestive, simply because of the endless combinations of products and possible marks.[64] Therefore, where a proposed trademark will fall on the spectrum, exactly, will depend primarily on the specific facts of each case.[65]

Fanciful marks are those which are specifically created for the purposes of source identification. In other words, fanciful marks are those which are newly created by the Seller for the sole purpose of representing his or her brand.[66] These marks have no actual meaning outside of their use as a mark.[67] These invented words or terms have no logical relation to the product itself, and do not describe any aspect of the product.[68] For example, "Häagen-Dazs," the famous ice cream brand, was created entirely from scratch without any real basis in any language.[69] Another example of a fanciful trademark is "Kodak"–it was created specifically to represent the Kodak camera brand.[70]

---

[64] *See* U.S. PAT. AND TRADEMARK OFF., *supra* note 63, § 1209.01(b).

[65] *Id.*

[66] *Id.* § 1209.01(a).

[67] *Id.*

[68] Lonnie E. Griffith et. al., 87 C.J.S. TRADEMARKS, ETC. § 204 (2018).

[69] Dan Nosowitz, *Häagen-Dazs Ice Cream Is From the Bronx—So What's With the Name?*, ATLAS OBSUCRA (Sept. 5, 2017), https://www.atlasobscura.com/articles/haagen-dazs-fake-foreign-branding (noting that, while Häagen-Dazs's founder wanted to create a name that sounded somewhat Danish, the trademark contains an umlaut, which is not present in Danish).

[70] Michael Zhang, *Origin and Evolution of Kodak's Name and Logo*, PETA PIXEL (Aug. 3, 2011), https://petapixel.com/2011/08/03/origin-and-evolution-of-kodaks-name-and-logo.

Arbitrary marks are similar to fanciful marks in a significant way: they do not relate to the product or describe any of its qualities.[71] Where a fanciful word has no dictionary meaning, an arbitrary mark is a common word which is being utilized in an uncommon way.[72] An example of an arbitrary mark is "Apple," when used as branding for tablets, computers, and phones. "Apple," though the common name of a popular fruit, does nothing to describe any electronic product on its own. Another example of an arbitrary mark is "Camel," which, when compared to the cigarette brand it promotes, is completely unrelated to the products it usually finds itself labeling.

A suggestive mark relates to the goods it is applied to only when the consumer must use his or her imagination to make a connection between the mark and the goods.[73] These marks do not openly describe or quantify certain characteristics of the goods, but instead only offer a point from which a consumer may relate the trademark to the goods with the "use [of] imagination or any type of multistage reasoning."[74] Examples of suggestive marks may include "Mountain Dew," which could evince the idea of a refreshing liquid, and "Microsoft," which could remind the consumer of either a microchip or software.

---

[71] U.S. PAT. AND TRADEMARK OFF., *supra* note 63, § 1209.01(a).
[72] Nautilus Group, Inc. v. Icon Health and Fitness, Inc., 372 F.3d 1330, 1340 (Fed. Cir. 2004).
[73] U.S. PAT. AND TRADEMARK OFF., *supra* note 63, § 1209.01(a).
[74] Entrepreneur Media, Inc. v. Smith, 279 F.2d 1135, 1142 (9th Cir. 2002) (quoting Kendall–Jackson Winery, Limited v. E. & J. Gallo Winery, 150 F.3d 1042, 1047 n. 8 (9th Cir. 1998)).

CJ's Tip: Of all the classifications a trademark may fall under, suggestive marks are perhaps the best to focus on creating for any Seller wishing to create both a strong brand which can both stand up to contentions and challenges of validity and be remembered easily by and stick in the minds of consumers. It is understandable and advisable that Sellers create a brand which is both inherently distinctive (more on that later) and allow the consumer to make a sensible connection between the trademark and the goods. Suggestive marks fulfill both of these aims; they afford consumers a leg to stand on in relating the mark to the product while at the same time remaining inherently distinctive so that registration and possible lawsuits challenging the mark's legitimacy do not offer much trouble.

Descriptive marks are those which "describe an ingredient, quality, characteristic, function, feature, purpose, or use of the specified goods."[75] In order to determine whether a mark is descriptive: does the mark signify or represent any quality or component of the subject goods.[76] Since these marks relate to the product, they are the second least-protectible type of mark in the hierarchy of distinctiveness. Examples of descriptive trademarks include "InkJoy," when in

---

[75] U.S. PAT. AND TRADEMARK OFF., *supra* note 63, § 1209.01(b).
[76] *Id.*

33

reference to a line of ballpoint pens, and "Windows," a computer operating system which features digital "windows" allowing users to view files and operate programs.[77]

Finally, at the bottom rung of the distinctiveness hierarchy are "generic marks." Generic marks include the word which the average consumer would recognize as the common name of the product itself.[78] Generic marks, because they are comprised of the actual word by which the product is known, can never be a trademark because they refer to the goods rather than the source.[79] Terms which could be considered generic may include "Salt," when affixed to packages filled with salt, or "Granite," when applied to a company which is solely engaged in the production and shipment of granite.

Also important in the discussion of the spectrum of distinctiveness is the concept of "inherent distinctiveness." A mark is inherently distinctive if its "intrinsic nature serves to identify a particular source of a product."[80] To determine whether a mark is inherently distinctive, the mark will be examined along a series of factors called the *Seabrook* factors, which are:

---

[77] Note that while "InkJoy" may not have acquired a secondary meaning and thus may not be protectible, "Windows" certainly has and thus is protectible. The concept of acquiring secondary meaning will be discussed in the following section of this chapter.

[78] U.S. PAT. AND TRADEMARK OFF., *supra* note 63, § 1209.01(c).

[79] *Id.*

[80] Two Pesos, Inc. v. Taco Cabana, Inc., 505 U.S. 763, 768 (1992).

34

(1) a "common" basic shape or design;

(2) unique or unusual in a particular field;

(3) a mere refinement of a commonly adopted and well-known form of ornamentation for a particular class of goods viewed by the public as a dress or ornamentation for the goods; or

(4) capable of creating a commercial impression distinct from the accompanying words.[81]

The *Seabrook* factors need not all be satisfied to deny a mark's inherent distinctiveness.[82] These are factors and not a strictly defined ruleset. The satisfaction of a single *Seabrook* factor can lead an examiner finding a lack of inherent distinctiveness in the subject mark. If the mark is found, based on the *Seabrook* factors, not to be inherently distinctive, it will either be denied registration or will not be protected if the mark is infringed by a third party.[83]

Where a mark resides on the spectrum of distinctiveness will determine how much protection it will be afforded as a trademark, or even if it can be considered a trademark. Where the mark falls will also determine whether it would likely be found to be inherently distinctive.

---

[81] U.S. PAT. AND TRADEMARK OFF., *supra* note 63, § 1202.02(b)(ii) (citing Seabrook Foods, Inc. v. Bar-Well Foods Limited, 568 F.2d 1342, 1344 (1977).
[82] *Id.* (citing *In re* Chippendales USA, Inc., 622 F.3d 1346, 1355 (Fed. Cir. 2010); *In re* Chevron Intellectual Prop. Grp. LLC, 96 U.S.P.Q.2d 2026, 2028 (TTAB 2010)).
[83] *Id.*

If arrayed onto a chart, the hierarchy of distinctive marks and the protections given to them would appear as the following:

Level of Distinctiveness	Protection
Fanciful	• Highest level of protection • Is presumed to be inherently distinctive • Registrable and protectible as a trademark
Arbitrary	• Is presumed to be inherently distinctive • Registrable and protectible as a trademark
Suggestive	• Will generally be presumed to be inherently distinctive unless its suggestive qualities run to close to describing the product • Registrable and protectible as a trademark
Descriptive	• Not presumed to be inherently distinctive • Can build and achieve a secondary meaning, by which consumers recognize the descriptive mark as really in fact relating to the Seller, only after which becoming a registrable and protectible trademark
Generic	• Lowest level of protection • Is never inherently distinctive and cannot build secondary meaning • Barred from ever becoming a registrable and protectible trademark

Anthony's Breakdown: Use the chart above to understand where your mark may fall. Suggestive and above, your mark will be inherently distinctive. Below, however, your mark will not be inherently distinctive. You'll need to either acquire secondary meaning if your mark is descriptive or your mark will never be distinctive enough and will thus never be registrable or protectible.

III.   Acquiring Secondary Meaning

One of the primary effects of a lack of inherent distinctiveness is that it will be barred from being listed in the Principal Register, although it may still be listed in the Supplemental Register. The Principal Register is a federal list of registered trademarks which grant presumptions of ownership in all 50 states, presumptions of trademark validity, and exclusive rights to use the mark.[84] In contrast, while the Supplemental Register allows the Seller to sue for infringement in federal court and protect his or her trademark in a localized area, the protection is not extended to the full 50 states, and it lacks the presumptions bestowed by the Principal Register.[85]

---

[84] Kelley Keller, *3 Biggest Differences Between the Principal Register and Supplemental Register for Trademarks*, KELLEY KELLER ESQ. (Feb. 2, 2018), http://kelleykeller.com/3-biggest-differences-principal-register-supplemental-register-trademarks.
[85] *Id.*

If a mark is not inherently distinctive, it must rely on acquiring secondary meaning to be registered on the Principal Register or to qualify for federal protection against infringement.[86] In other words, a Seller with a mark which is not inherently distinctive must demonstrate that the mark has come to reference himself or herself and not just the product to the general consuming public.[87] Without such a secondary meaning, a mark which is not inherently distinctive will be denied both registration or redressability for infringement.[88]

Under the Lanham Act, there are several types of evidence which may be accepted and reviewed to support the contention that the Seller's mark has acquired a secondary meaning.[89] This list of possible evidence includes: (1) the prior registration of the same or similar mark on the Principal Register; (2) the use of the mark in commerce for a period of at least five years; and (3) other evidence which would be appropriate and pertinent to finding a secondary meaning. "Other evidence" includes the extent and success of advertisements using the mark, affidavits or declarations asserting that the mark is recognized as a source indicator, and surveys, market research, and consumer studies.[90]

---

[86] *See* U.S. PAT. AND TRADEMARK OFF., *supra* note 63, § 1212.
[87] *Id.* (quoting Ralston Purina Co. v. Thomas J. Lipton, Inc., 341 F. Supp. 129, 133 (S.D.N.Y. 1972)).
[88] *Id.*
[89] 15 U.S.C. § 1052(f) (2016).
[90] *Id.*; U.S. PAT. AND TRADEMARK OFF., *supra* note 63, § 1212.06(b)–(d).

Under § 1052(f) of the Lanham Act, evidence of acquired secondary meaning may be supplied along with the initial application to the examiner.[91] If, however, the Seller's mark has already been denied registration by the examiner, the Seller may appeal the decision by submitting a claim that the mark has acquired secondary meaning. This claim is called "acquired distinctiveness in the alternative."[92] This appeal will basically be reviewed in the same way as if the claim of secondary meaning had been submitted initially with the application. Accordingly, the examiner will rely on the same types of evidence the Seller would submit with a normal claim of secondary meaning.[93]

Without inherent distinctiveness, a Seller may find that his or her mark is eligible to be registered on the Supplemental Register. To reiterate, although it is not the Principal Register, the Supplemental Register allows for multiple benefits in addition to those from simply using the mark in commerce.[94] These benefits include: the right to bring infringement suits in federal court; preclusion of the registration of similar marks which are confusing to the Seller's mark; protection in other countries on the basis of international treaties; and strong evidence

---

[91] *See* 15 U.S.C. § 1052.
[92] U.S. PAT. AND TRADEMARK OFF., *supra* note 63, § 1212.06(c).
[93] *Id.*
[94] Matthew D. Asbell, *Inherent and Acquired Distinctiveness and The Principal and Supplemental Registers for U.S. Trademarks*, LADAS & PARRY (May 1, 2014), https://ladas.com/education-center/inherent-acquired-distinctiveness-principal-supplemental-registers-u-s-trademarks.

for acceptance onto the Principal Register.[95] Those who file their marks on the Supplemental Register are unable to switch their registration to be placed on the Principal Register, but may file an independent application to be registered on the Principal Register once inherent distinctiveness has been achieved and five years of continued use in commerce has passed.

IV.   Genericide

The last concept to bear in mind when designing or choosing a trademark is the unfortunate occurrence of "genericide." Under the Lanham Act, "[a]t any time if the registered mark becomes the generic name for the goods" then the trademark may be challenged via a petition to cancel the mark.[96] In other words, a trademark will lose its protection if it becomes the actual name of the product rather than a reference to the Seller in the eyes of the consuming public.[97] Examples of trademarks which have been killed by genericide include such recognizable words as "yo-yo," "escalator," "aspirin," and "thermos."[98] Other brands are right on the cusp of genericide and are fighting frantically to keep their trademarks, sometimes with mixed results. For

---

[95] *Id.* (noting that those on the Supplemental Register lack many of the protections garnered by being placed on the Principal Register, including access to the Madrid Protocol, filing with U.S. Customs to prevent importation of infringing products, having the date of constructive use relate back to the filing date of the application, and constructive notice to others of the trademark's priority).

[96] 15 U.S.C. 1064(3) (2016).

[97] *Id.*

[98] John Dwight Ingram, *The Genericide of Trademarks*, 2 BUFF. INTELL. PROP. L.J. 154, 154 (2004).

example, Velcro, the producer of a particular type of fasteners, has recently begun pleading to consumers not to use their "VELCRO" trademark as a noun, verb, or adjective to avoid their mark becoming generic. According to them, the correct name for their fasteners is not "velcro strips," but instead "hook-and-loop fasteners."[99]

There is no standard ordained by the Lanham Act to determine whether a trademark has been the victim of genericide.[100] Instead, case law has established the precedent of the "public perception" test, which asks: "What do the buyers understand by the word for whose use the parties are contending?"[101] This is, therefore, a situation a Seller needs to be wary of if their trademark has superseded the originally generic term in describing the product. When this happens, the trademark

---

[99] Jack Neff, *Velcro Targets Trademark Abusers Again with Singing Lawyers,* ADAGE (June 5, 2018), http://adage.com/article/cmo-strategy/velcro-trademark-abusers-singing-lawyers/313735/.
[100] *Id.* at 156.
[101] *Id.* at 156-57 (quoting Bayer Co. v. United Drug Co., 272 F. 505, 509 (S.D.N.Y. 1921)).

describes the product, not the Seller. This is especially bothersome for sellers who hold a patent in their product and are thus able to prevent the manufacture and sale of said products for a period of 20 years, during which time the consuming public may have come to associate the trademark with the product itself.[102] Genericide can also be an unintended and unfortunate outcome of success.[103] It is, essentially, an eventual penalty for successfully marketing and imprinting the Seller's trademark into the minds of consumers.[104]

To avoid genericide, Sellers can employ a number of tactics to prevent their trademark from becoming the generic term for the product. First, if the product is one the Seller has invented and patented, the Seller should also introduce a generic term for the product which differs from the trademark.[105] Second, Sellers should never use their trademarks as nouns or verbs.[106] Third, Sellers should remain vigilant and proactive in protecting their brands and policing their use as verbs and nouns by third parties.[107] In short, if the Seller treats his or her trademark as a trademark designating the origin of the product and not the name or function of the product itself, Sellers can generally escape the specter of genericide.

---

[102] *Id.* at 158-59.
[103] *Id.* at 159.
[104] *Id.*
[105] *Id.*
[106] *Id.* at 160.
[107] *Id.*

CHAPTER 4: TRADE DRESS

I. Introduction

Trade dress is a form of intellectual property that is protected under the Lanham Act and has been defined by the Supreme Court as the "total image and overall appearance" of a good.[108] Under the traditional view, trade dress only protected the way a product was "dressed up" and sold in the market.[109] The modern standard of trade dress established by the Court finds features such as size, shape, color or color combinations, texture, graphics, and particular sales techniques protectible under the concept of trade dress.[110]

Almost any distinctive component of a product or service can be protected by trade dress. However, the principal categories of trade dress are:

(1) product packaging;

(2) product design;

(3) color;

(4) business exteriors and interiors; and,

(5) sounds and scents.[111]

---

[108] John H. Harland Co. v. Clarke Checks, Inc., 711 F.2d 966, 980 (11th Cir. 1983).
[109] Jeffrey Milstein, Inc. v. Greger, Lawlor, Roth, Inc., 58 F.3d 27, 31 (2d Cir. 1995).
[110] *Harland Co.*, 711 F.2d at 980.
[111] Practical Law Intellectual Property & Technology, *Trade Dress Protection*, THOMSON REUTERS (2018).

The process for evaluating a product's trade dress differs based on whether the feature is inherently distinctive or not.

In order to prevail in a trade dress infringement action under the Lanham Act § 43(a), a Seller must prove: (1) that the feature is non-functional; (2) that it's mark is distinctive; and (3) that a likelihood of confusion exists between the Seller's product and the infringer's product.[112]

Enforcing trade dress in court begins with the Seller drafting an inclusive complaint that includes all important features and elements of their product that they want protected under trade dress. Other considerations include whether the trade dress is registered or unregistered, whether the product's feature is being infringed or diluted, and what relief is available to the Seller.

II.   Protectability

Section 43(a) of the Lanham Act protects both registered and unregistered trade dress. Protection under § 43(a) requires that the trade dress must be non-functional and distinctive.[113]

---

[112] Two Pesos, Inc. v. Taco Cabana, Inc., 505 U.S. 763, 769 (1992).
[113] 15 U.S.C. § 1125 (2016).

A functional feature of a product is a feature which gives the customer an actual benefit, rather than just assurance that it is from a particular producer.[114] This means that the feature is part of the product, not part of the branding.

When determining if the feature is functional or non-functional, courts evaluate whether the feature is essential to the use or purpose of the product or to the cost or quality of the good.[115] For example, the spherical shape of a soccer ball is imperative for its use in playing soccer. However, the color or design on a soccer ball could amount to trade dress because these would be non-functional features. This is because the color or design on a soccer ball is not an essential feature to its purpose and could easily be changed without inhibiting its primary use.

Courts have ruled that functional product features are not protected under the Lanham Act.[116] The purpose of the functionality doctrine is to prevent Sellers from developing monopolies by obtaining trademark protection for the functional feature of a product and effectively eliminating the possibility of competition.[117] The Ninth Circuit has recognized two factors for determining if features are

---

[114] Joel W. Reese, *Defining the Elements of Trade Dress Infringement Under Section 43(a) of the Lanham Act*, 2 TEX. INTELL. PROP. L.J. 103, 115 (1994) (quoting International Order of Job's Daughters v. Lindeburg & Co., 633 F.2d 912, 917 (9th Cir. 1980), cert. denied, 452 U.S. 941 (1981)).
[115] *Id.*
[116] TrafFix Devices, Inc. v. Mktg. Displays, Inc., 532 U.S. 23, 29 (2001).
[117] Standard Terry Mills, Inc. v. Shen Mfg. Co., 803 F.2d 778, 781 (3d Cir. 1986).

functional: (1) the availability of alternative designs and (2) whether the particular design comes from a simple or cheap manufacturing method.[118]

> CJ's Tip: The important thing to keep in mind regarding functionality is whether you are trying to trademark the purpose of the product you are selling or simply as the design or aspect of the good that is not important to its use.

To establish non-functionality, one must prove that the feature of the product does not affect competition. Functionality is defined by the following two concepts:

(1) the utilitarian functionality test and

(2) the aesthetic functionality test.[119]

The utilitarian test focuses on whether the design or feature of the product gives the manufacturer a cost advantage for production, shipping, or other related expenses. The utilitarian functionality test, also known as the *Inwood* test, established that the Supreme Court deems a product feature to be functional if it is essential to the use or purpose of the trade or affects the cost or quality of the good.[120] For

---

[118] Sega Enterprises Ltd. v. Accolade, Inc., 977 F.2d 1510, 1531 (1992).
[119] Reese, *supra* note 114, at 117.
[120] Inwood Labs., Inc. v. Ives Labs., Inc., 456 U.S. 844, 850 (1982).

example, the design of an x-frame foldable chair has been ruled as functional because the product is designed that way only to be a more efficient chair, not so the consumer will recognize the company who produced it.[121] Therefore, it fits the utilitarian functionality test because the design is essential for the purpose of the chair rather than to distinguish the product from competitors. *In re Becton, Dickinson and Co.* evaluated whether the design of a cap for blood collection tubes was functional and determined that the cost was not a factor because the design of the cap did not lower manufacturing costs.[122]

If the design is not functional based on the *Inwood* test, it must still pass the test established in *Qualitex Co. v. Jacobson Products Co., Inc.* In *Qualitex*, the Supreme Court created the "aesthetic functionality" test by ruling a feature is functional where exclusive use of the feature would put competitors at a significant non-reputation-related disadvantage.[123] The Supreme Court in *TrafFix Devices, Inc. v. Mktg. Displays, Inc.* clarified that the aesthetic functionality test need not be considered where the challenged product is functional under the utilitarian functionality test.[124] Once the functionality of the product's feature has been evaluated, one must analyze the distinctiveness of the product's feature based on the tests discussed in the previous chapter.

---

[121] Specialized Seating, Inc. v. Greenwich Industries, LP, 616 F.3d 722, 727 (2010).
[122] *In re* Becton, Dickinson and Co., 675 F.3d 1368, 1376 (2012).
[123] Qualitex Co. v. Jacobson Products Co., Inc., 514 U.S. 159, 165 (1995).
[124] Practical Law Intellectual Property & Technology, *supra* note 111.

The aesthetic test addresses features that are solely ornamental but are essential to effective competition.

III.　Trade Dress Categories

The most prevalent category of trade dress is product packaging. Packaging covered by trade dress can include labeling, wrappers, cartons, containers, unique shape, and more.

In *Paddington Corp. v. Attiki Importers & Distributors, Inc.*, a Court examined the importance of product packaging and evaluated what will constitute trade dress. First, is the packaging inherently distinctive or not.[125] If the packaging is inherently distinctive, the court will only need to look at the likelihood of confusion. If the packaging is not inherently distinctive, the court evaluates whether the packaging is the custom in the industry. For example, packaging cereal in a rectangular shaped box is such common practice amongst cereal companies that no one brand would be able to claim trade dress for the shape of the common cereal box. However, without the common

---

[125] Paddington Corp. v. Attic Importers & Distributors, Inc., 996 F.2d 577, 583 (1993).

industry practice, the shape of a box could be suggestive or arbitrary and therefore inherently distinctive.[126]

The design of the product is another important feature protected by trade dress that includes the product's configuration. Trade dress as product design is incapable of being inherently distinctive and the Seller must provide proof of "secondary meaning."[127] For example, the three stripes on Adidas sneakers constitute a product design protected by trade dress because it has acquired secondary meaning.[128]

A color combination on the product may rise to the level of being

protected by trade dress. In *Qualitex*, the Supreme Court established the standard that even a single color can be protected.[129] For example, a specific color used in connection with fiberglass insulation products that has no functional purpose, does not decrease manufacturing costs, and

---

[126] *Id.*
[127] Adidas-Salomon AG v. Target Corp., 228 F.Supp.2d 1192 (D. Or. 2002).
[128] *Id.*
[129] *Qualitex*, 514 U.S. at 159.

is solely used to identify the source of the goods, is protectible by trade dress.[130]

The exterior and interior elements of a business, such as restaurants or other commercial businesses, can be protected by trade dress. The standard for this category was set out in a case called *Two Pesos, Inc. v. Taco Cabana, Inc.* In the Two Pesos case, one restaurant claimed another restaurant infringed on its' trade dress by closely copying the festive atmosphere and decorative designs. The Court ruled that restaurant layouts such as food preparation areas visible to customers, storage items visible to customers, the tiles on the wall, mirrors placement, and types of chairs can be protected by trade dress.[131]

The final category of trade dress protects sounds and scents of a particular good. For example, the USPTO has given trademarks to the scent of yarn[132] and to the NBC chime sound[133].

IV.   Trade Dress Enforcement under the Lanham Act

The enforcement of trade dress is similar to the enforcement of trademarks.   The Lanham Act protects against infringement of

---

[130] *In re* Owens-Corning Fiberglas Corp., 774 F.2d 1116, 1124 (Fed. Cir. 1985).
[131] Fuddruckers, Inc. v. Doc's B.R. Others, Inc., 826 F.2d 837, 839 (9th Cir. 1987).
[132] *In re* Clarke, 17 U.S.P.Q.2d 1238 (T.T.A.B. 1990).
[133] U.S. Trademark Registration No. 916,522 (Defining the NBC Chime sound as "the musical notes G, E, C, played on chimes").

registered or unregistered trade dress and trade dress dilution.[134] Registered trade dress infringement is covered by § 32 of the Lanham Act, while unregistered trade dress infringement is covered by § 43(a). However, most trade dress infringement actions involve cases where the product has not been registered for trade dress.

The basic test for determining whether unregistered trade dress infringement has occurred is whether there is a "likelihood of confusion." Under § 43(a) of the Lanham Act, the likelihood of confusion standard is

> [I]f the infringing trademark or trade dress is likely to cause confusion, or to cause mistake, or to deceive as to the affiliation, connection, or association of such person with another person, or as to the origin, sponsorship, or approval of his or her goods, services, or commercial activities by another person.[135]

The act does not expressly say whom the likelihood of confusion must apply to, but most federal jurisdictions have favored confusion for the general public rather than potential customers of a manufacturer or

---

[134] Practical Law Intellectual Property & Technology, *supra* note 111.
[135] Reese, *supra* note 114, at 117.

business.[136] The factors for likelihood of confusion are the same as the previous chapter.

When drafting a lawsuit, the Seller must clearly express the specific features of the product that is covered by trade dress. This allows the court to assess the protectability of the trade dress and award narrowly-tailored relief.[137] Therefore, sellers frequently define trade dress as the features being copied by the defendant.

> Anthony's Advice: When drafting your complaint, make sure you identify the proper number of elements to be covered by trade dress. It is very hard to change your definition of trade dress during future proceedings. If you fail to list all the elements of trade dress related to your product, you subject yourself to other competitors

---

[136] *Id.*

[137] Landscape Forms, Inc. v. Columbia Cascade Co., 113 F.3d 373, 381 (2d Cir. 1997).

stealing the unlisted elements in the future. If too many elements are listed, the defendant will be able to avoid the injunction by only changing a few of the elements and not all of them.

Another important factor to consider when suing for trade dress infringement is the burden of proving non-functionality is on the plaintiff.[138] Therefore, Sellers asserting a trade dress infringement complaint need to prove the features included in the complaint are non-functional. However, for trade dress that is registered, the trade dress is presumed to be non-functional and the defendant has the burden of proving functionality.[139]

Trade dress dilution is addressed in § 43(c) of the Lanham Act, which covers blurring or tarnishing of a mark.[140] If the trade dress is not registered, a Seller must prove in a dilution action that: (1) the claimed trade dress, taken as a whole, is not functional and is famous and (2) if the claimed trade dress includes a mark or marks registered on the principal register, the unregistered matter, taken as a whole, is well-known, separate, and apart from any fame of the registered marks.[141]

---

[138] Practical Law Intellectual Property & Technology, *supra* note 111.
[139] Aromatique, Inc. v. Gold Seal, Inc., 28 F.3d 863, 869 (8th Cir. 1994).
[140] Practical Law Intellectual Property & Technology, *supra* note 111.
[141] *Id.*

The principal forms of relief and defenses to a trade dress claim are below:

Principal Relief for Trade Dress Claims	Principal Defenses for Trade Dress Claims
1. Injunctive relief 2. Actual damages (may be enhanced up to three times the actual amount in certain circumstances) 3. An award of the infringer's profits 4. Attorney's fees 5. Destruction of infringing articles 6. Product recall	1. Functionality Defense 2. Preemption of State law claims

CHAPTER 5 – LIKELIHOOD OF CONFUSION

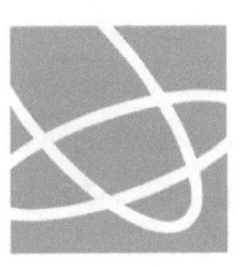 

I.   Introduction

Once a Seller creates a registrable and protectible trademark, an issue that arises is maintaining the sole use of that mark. A trademark is a mark of assurance to the buyer of the product's point of origin.

There are, unfortunately, a large number of people and businesses that try and hijack reputable Sellers' products. One of the easiest ways for competitors hijack Private Label Sellers' products is to infringe on their trademark.

The USPTO defines trademark infringement as "the unauthorized use of a trademark or service mark on or in connection with goods and/or services in a manner that is likely to cause confusion, deception, or mistake about the source of the goods and/or services."[142]

---

[142] *About Trademark Infringement*, USPTO (last visited July 16, 2018), https://www.uspto.gov/page/about-trademark-infringement.

Through trademark infringement, hijackers fool buyers into believing that the goods they are purchasing are coming from the Private Label Seller or brand which provides better products and services to buyers. In effect, hijackers steal business from Sellers. Infringers damage the reputation of the Seller's brand by having consumers associate the Seller's brand with sub-standard goods.

The Lanham Act allows for aggrieved Sellers who own marks to seek damages in civil lawsuits against infringers. Specifically, a hijacker who infringes on Private Label Sellers' marks in commerce is liable if the infringement is:

> likely to cause confusion, or to cause mistake, or to deceive as the affiliation, connection, or association of such [seller] with another [seller], or as to the origin, sponsorship, or approval of his or her goods, services, or commercial activities by another [seller] . . . shall be liable in a civil action by any [seller] who believes that he or she is or is likely to be damaged by such act.[143]

In other words, if a Seller's trademark is infringed upon, the Seller can sue the infringer.

---

[143] 15 U.S.C. § 1125(a)(2).

CJ's Side Note: This chapter is important not only to be aware of when you can bring a lawsuit for trademark infringement, but also to offer you a set of guidelines to evaluate whether someone is violating your rights and to help avoid infringing on another's intellectual property rights. The law, the Lanham Act, does not differentiate between those who intentionally or mistakenly infringe.

II.   Confusion Among Consumers

When the Court is determining whether a certain trademark infringes upon another, it must first determine whether there is a likelihood of confusion between the two marks.[144] The focal point of

confusion in trademark infringement cases is the consumer. The consumer is the party which may be influenced by the trademark and

---

[144] *See id.*

the inherent assurances and guarantees of quality therein to ultimately make a purchase.[145]

The Federal Court uses what are called the *du Pont* factors to determine whether there is a likelihood of confusion between two competing marks.[146] The list of factors, as described by the Court, are:

(1) The similarity or dissimilarity of the marks in their entireties as to appearance, sound, connotation and commercial impression

(2) The similarity or dissimilarity and nature of the goods or services as described in an application or registration or in connection with which a prior mark is in use

(3) The similarity or dissimilarity of established, likely-to-continue trade channels

(4) The conditions under which and buyers to whom sales are made, i.e. "impulse" vs. careful, sophisticated purchasing

(5) The fame of the prior mark (sales, advertising, length of use)

---

[145] *See* Jeff Pietsch, *Trademark Infringement: Factors Considered in Consumer Confusion*, THE IP LAW BLOG (May 9, 2007), https://www.theiplawblog.com/2007/05/articles/trademark-law/trademark-infringement-factors-considered-in-consumer-confusion; Tiffany Valeriano, *7 Factors for Identifying Trademark Likelihood of Confusion*, TRADEMARK NOW (Mar. 28, 2017), https://www.trademarknow.com/blog/7-factors-for-identifying-trademark-likelihood-of-confusion.
[146] J. THOMAS McCARTHY, 4 McCARTHY ON TRADEMARKS AND UNFAIR COMPETITION § 24:43 (5th ed.) (2018).

(6) The number and nature of similar marks in use on similar goods

(7) The nature and extent of any actual confusion

(8) The length of time during and conditions under which there has been concurrent use without evidence of actual confusion

(9) The variety of goods on which a mark is or is not used (house mark, "family" mark, product mark)

(10) The market interface between applicant and the owner of a prior mark:

   a. a mere "consent" to register or use

   b. agreement provisions designed to preclude confusion, i.e. limitations on continued use of the marks by each party

   c. assignment of mark, application, registration and good will of the related business

   d. laches and estoppel attributable to owner of prior mark and indicative of lack of confusion

   e. The extent to which applicant has a right to exclude others from use of its mark on its goods

(11) The extent of potential confusion, i.e., whether de minimis or substantial

(12) Any other established fact probative of the effect
of use.[147]

All of the factors do not need to be met. They are factors for
consideration, not a checklist. Not all factors will be relevant in all
cases. In an evaluation, only the factors at issue will be considered in
reaching the ultimate determination of infringement.[148] As a fact-
specific set of factors, *du Pont* requires every case to follow a new and
distinct weighting for each factor in light of the case's circumstances.[149]
Even a minority of factors, regardless of the magnitude, may be the sole
focus of discussion if these specific factors could on their own decide or
control the case.[150] However, of particular importance is the similarity
or dissimilarity of both the trademarks and the goods in question.[151]

Answering the first *du Pont* factor: the similarity or dissimilarity
of the marks, may solve the issue of the likelihood of confusion on its
own.[152] In fact, the similarity or dissimilarity of the marks in question
have been held to hold a place of high determination when viewed in
connection with likelihood of confusion. It has been repeatedly noted

[147] *In re* E.I. Du Pont de Nemours & Co., 476 F.2d 1357, 1361 (C.C.P.A. 1973).
[148] McCARTHY, *supra* note 146 § 14:43.
[149] *In re* Mighty Leaf Tea, 601 F.3d 1342, 1346 (Fed. Cir. 2010).
[150] *See* Citigroup Inc. v. Capital City Bank Group, Inc., 637 F.3d 1344, 1354-55
(Fed. Cir. 2011) (ruling that the T.T.A.B. did not err in only considering six of the
thirteen *du Pont* factors relevant in determining a likelihood of confusion) (quoting
In re Majestic Distilling Co., 315 F.3d 1311, 1315 (Fed. Cir. 2003)).
[151] *In re* SL&E Training Stable, Inc., 2008 WL 4107225, *2 (T.T.A.B. 2008).
[152] *Id.*; Odom's Tenn. Pride Sausage, Inc. v. FF Acquisition, L.L.C., 600 F.3d 1343,
1346-47 (Fed. Cir. 2010).

that cases may be decided on this factor alone.[153] In most cases, as long as the marks are so different in "appearance, sound, connotation and commercial impression" that there cannot be any possibility that there would exist a likelihood of confusion, summary judgment will be granted to the party accused of infringement.[154]

> Anthony's Breakdown: Summary judgment is a fancy legal term for when one side is given an automatic victory over the other side in a legal proceeding. It is a fast track to skip the trouble and cost of a trial and reach a definite decision early in the case. Whether you are a Seller who has brought a lawsuit against someone who has infringed on your trademark or one who is accused of violating someone's trademark, you want to obtain summary judgment in your favor.

The question of whether the two marks in question seem similar or dissimilar is predicated upon the "recollection of the average purchaser, who normally retains a general rather than a specific impression of trademarks," not a "side-by-side comparison."[155] In

---

[153] *See* Odom's Tenn. Pride Sausage, Inc., 600 F.3d at 1346-47; Champagne Louis Roederer v. Delicato Vineyards, 148 F.3d 1373, 1375 (Fed. Cir. 1998) (citing Kellogg Co. v. Pack'em Enters., 951 F.2d 330, 332-33 (Fed. Cir. 1991); Keebler Co. v. Murray Bakery Prods., 866 F.2d 1386, 1388 (Fed. Cir. 1989)).
[154] Kellogg Co., 951 F.2d at 332 (quoting Du Pont de Nemours & Co., 476 F.2d at 1361).
[155] Barbara's Bakery, Inc. v. Barbara Landesman, 2007 WL 196406, *5 (T.T.A.B. 2007).

addition, the examining judge has full authority to give greater credence to one feature of a trademark if it has a substantial amount of significance as compared to the trademark as a whole.[156] Further, the second *du Pont* factor, the similarity or dissimilarity of the goods sold under the trademarks in question, have great influence over the likelihood of confusion between the trademarks themselves. If the goods sold under both trademarks are completely or nearly identical, the extent of similarity between the two trademarks which must exist before the court finds of a likelihood of confusion is substantially lessened.[157]

The similarity or dissimilarity of the subject goods are just as important as the similarity or dissimilarity of the trademarks in determining the presence of a likelihood of confusion. Of the degree of similarity between the goods sold under the contending marks:

> [t]he authority is legion that the question of registrability of an applicant's mark must be decided on the basis of the identification of goods set forth in the application regardless of what the record may reveal as to the particular nature of an applicant's goods, the particular channels of trade or the class of purchasers to which sales of the goods are directed.[158]

---

[156] *Id.*

[157] *Id.*

[158] Octocom Systems, Inc. v. Houston Computer Services, Inc., 918 F.2d 937, 942 (Fed. Cir. 1990) (citing Squirtco v. Tomy Corp., 697 F.2d 1038, 1042 (Fed. Cir. 1983); Tuxedo Monopoly, Inc. v. General Mills Fun Group, Inc., 648 F.2d 1335, 1337 (C.C.P.A. 1981); San Fernando Elec. Mfg. Co. v. JFD Elecs. Components Corp., 565 F.2d 683, 684–85 (C.C.P.A. 1977)).

For example, in a case regarding the likelihood of confusion between two marks, the fact that both parties were involved in the sale of bags, especially luggage, wallets, and handbags, was one of the deciding factors in finding a likelihood of confusion, even though one party's product offerings went beyond bags and included tanned leather for upholstery, umbrellas, and harnesses.[159] The Court reasoned that there was no restriction for the scope of the applicant's goods, and so they encompassed the registrant's goods.[160]

Courts may also examine the similarity or dissimilarity of the trade channels of the two competing marks. "Trade channels" refer to the environment or locale in which the products bearing the competing trademarks will be sold.[161] When competing trademarks share a trade channel overlap, there exists a higher likelihood that a consumer will confuse the two marks, an effect compounded by any existing similarity between the marks and the labeled products.[162] For example, the court may find that two pharmaceutical products which will both be sold in drug stores or supermarkets with a pharmacy department may lead to a greater likelihood of confusion between consumers.[163]

---

[159] *In re* SL&E Training Stable, Inc., 2008 WL 4107225, *2, *6 (T.T.A.B. 2008).
[160] *Id.* at *2.
[161] Anne Gilson LaLonde, *Proving Ownership Online ... and Keeping It: The Internet's Impact on Trademark Use and Coexistence*, 104 TRADEMARK REP. 1275, 1317 (2014).
[162] *Id.*
[163] *See* Allergan, Inc. v. KRL Group, Inc., 2013 WL 5946235, *5 (T.T.A.B. 2013).

For the Seller, the question will generally be whether a consumer may be able to encounter both parties' goods online, especially if the goods can both be found on the same webpage or website.[164] Some judicial decisions, however, have ruled that products being sold on the internet on separate retail platforms would be considered as occupying the same trade channel (e.g. the internet), regardless of their platform of origin.[165] These decisions are rare, however, and in most cases the items sold on large online retailers, such as Amazon, will not be found to inhabit the same trade channel. After all, most, if not all, goods may be bought on Amazon by virtue of the retailer monolith's size alone.[166] The similarity of goods, therefore, as well as their location *within* the website, have great influence over whether goods being sold online can be found within the same trade channel.[167]

A Federal Court has held that the mark's fame, the fifth *du Pont* factor, will control when the matter involves an exceptionally famous trademark.[168] Such famous trademarks are made famous through the use of distinctive design, a great amount of advertising and promotion, and noteworthy products.[169] The incentives created by emulating famous trademarks, as well as the amount of consumers who may be

---

[164] LaLonde, *supra* note 161, at 1317.

[165] *Id.* at 318.

[166] *Id.* at 1321 (citing *In re* MDG Tools, Inc., 2010 TTAB LEXIS 230 (T.T.A.B. 2010)).

[167] *Id.* at 1319, 1322.

[168] *See* Kenner Parker Toys Inc. v. Rose Art Industries, Inc., 963 F.2d 350, 352 (Fed. Cir. 1992).

[169] *Id.* at 353.

defrauded by the emulation of such marks, affords them an enhanced amount of legal protection when compared to lesser-known marks.[170] In general, Courts find that well-known marks' fame must always be considered as being more likely to persuade a purchaser to buy the product rather than a relatively unknown mark. The trademark which looks like a famous mark will more easily confuse the purchaser than one which looks like an unknown mark.[171] A seller who is creating or drafting a trademark should, therefore, be cautious to ensure that his or her mark does not approach the line of seeming similar to a particularly famous trademark.

Actual evidence of past confusion between two marks is highly indicative of there being a likelihood of confusion.[172] The fact that consumers have been confused by two competing trademarks in the past is definitely one of the most important of the *du Pont* factors in determining whether a likelihood of confusion exists. In fact, some courts have ruled that such evidence of actual confusion will create an inference of a likelihood of confusion alone.[173] Such evidence of actual confusion could include testimony or records of consumers who made mistaken purchases, misdirected communications, or open inquiries into relationships between the parties and the goods.[174]

---

[170] *Id.* at 352-53.
[171] *Id.* at 353 (quoting Specialty Brands v. Coffee Bean Distribs., 748 F.2d 669, 675 (Fed. Cir. 1984)).
[172] Michael J. Allen, *The Role of Actual Confusion Evidence in Trademark Infringement Litigation*, 83 TRADEMARK REP. 267, 269 (1993).
[173] *Id.*
[174] *See id.* at 274.

CHAPTER 6: FAIR USE OF ANOTHER'S TRADEMARK

I.   Introduction

"Fair Use" is a legal term that delineates when you can use another's trademark and when another person or company can use your trademark. There are two forms of "fair use."

Definitions: The first type of fair use is known as "classic" or "descriptive" fair use. Descriptive fair use is where the trademark is being used to describe the Seller's goods or services, geographic origin or the owner of the business.[175] The other type is called a "nominative fair use." A nominative fair use occurs when someone uses another's trademark without any likelihood of confusion as to the identity of the original owner.[176] The term "junior user" refers to the person or business that is using someone else's mark.

Classic and nominative fair use can be distinguished by several factors, such as: (1) the way in which the trademark is being used and (2) how to determine if the junior user is using the mark legally. The Ninth Circuit has defined the different situations in which the types of fair use should be used; "[t]he nominative fair use analysis is appropriate where a defendant has used the plaintiff's mark to describe the plaintiff's product, even if the defendant's ultimate goal is to describe

---

[175] J. THOMAS MCCARTHY, *supra* note 146, § 23:11.
[176] *Id.*

his own product. Conversely, the classic fair use analysis is appropriate where a defendant has used the plaintiff's mark only to describe his own product, and not at all to describe the plaintiff's product."[177]

II. Classic Fair Use

Classic fair use under § 33(b)(4) of the Lanham Act is when a junior user uses language or images that resemble the trademark owner's to *describe* his own product or service.[178]

The elements of proving the classic fair use defense are: (1) junior user's use of the term is not as a trademark or service mark; (2) junior user uses the term "fairly and in good faith;" and (3) junior user uses the term only to describe its goods or services.[179] An example of a classic fair use dispute would be a company using "sweet-tart" to describe a juice flavor. This does not infringe on the trademark "Sweet-tarts" for the candy company.[180] In this case, the juice company sells a variety of flavored juices that they advertise as being sweet and tart, often phrasing it as "sweet-tart."[181] The company that produces the sweet-tart candy was unhappy with the hyphenated structure of the advertisement and sought an injunction against the juice company for trademark infringement.

---

[177] Cairns v. Franklin Mint Co., 292 F.3d 1139, 1151 (9th Cir. 2002).
[178] Stephanie M. Greene, *Sorting Out "Fair Use" and "Likelihood of Confusion" in Trademark Law*, 43 AM. BUS. L.J. 43, 50 (2006).
[179] *Cairns*, 292 F.3d at 1151.
[180] Sunmark, Inc. v. Ocean Spray Cranberries, Inc., 64 F.3d 1055 (7th Cir. 1995).
[181] *Id.* at 1057.

To evaluate whether this constitutes trademark infringement, the facts need to be applied to the test for the classic fair use defense. The

first element requires that the term is not being used as a trademark by the juice company. According to the facts given, the juice company is simply using the term to describe their own product. They are not attempting to use the sweet-tart brand to promote their own product or make it appear as if they have any connection with the sweet-tart brand. Instead, they are only trying to use the words sweet and tart to describe the flavor of the juice.

The second element in determining classic fair use is whether the use of the term is fair and in good faith. In this case, there is no indication the term was being used in bad faith. For this to occur, a junior user would have to be actively trying to use the trademark to promote their product. The juice company is using the words in a descriptive manner; they are not using the trademark or the sweet-tart brand in any fashion to promote the juice.

Finally, the last element of the classic fair use test is whether the junior user used the term to describe their own product or services. The juice company satisfies this element because they used sweet-tart to describe the taste of their juice.

The purpose of the classic fair use defense is avoid prohibiting competitors from using language that is needed to describe their products or services. Therefore, when companies acquire a trademark they do not have the exclusive right to use the English language words included in the trademark. It is impractical for only the candy company to be allowed to use the words "sweet" and "tart" for commercial purposes which would create unfair competition.

In contrast, an example that would not fit the third element of the classic fair use test would be where two manufacturers of baseball bats used the term "Slugger" to identify a baseball bat that hits harder than other baseball bats.
If one manufacturer has trademark protections for the term, the junior user will not be able to argue nominative fair use because slugger is not a descriptive word for the bat. This is because the term slugger is not being used to describe anything to do with the bat. It does not describe the make, design, color, material or anything other aspect of the bat. It is simply used to identify a specific bat. Since classic fair use only applies for descriptive purposes, the junior user would not be protected by this defense.

Anthony's Breakdown: A useful way to understand whether classic fair use would be acceptable is whether it is a descriptive word you are using. Words that have no descriptive purpose, such as "Starbucks," "Gatorade," or "iPhone" will not be protected by classic fair use. This is because these terms are specific for identifying the brand they are registered for trademark by and do not serve any descriptive purpose of the good. Terms such as "latte," "sports drink," or "apple" are descriptive.

III.   Nominative Fair Use

Fair use disputes more commonly address the nominative fair use of another's trademark. Nominative fair use is where a junior user employs the trademark to identify the trademark owner's goods or services.[182] As long as there is no likelihood of confusion, this will not be trademark infringement.

The Ninth Circuit has established the three elements for nominative fair use:

(1) the plaintiff's product or service in question must be one not readily identifiable without use of the trademark;

---

[182] J. THOMAS MCCARTHY, *supra* note 146, § 23:11.

(2) only so much of the mark or marks may be used as is reasonably necessary to identify the plaintiff's product or service, and;

(3) the user must do nothing that would, in conjunction with the mark, suggest sponsorship or endorsement by the trademark holder.[183]

Consider the example of a famous television host who loaned his name to a commercial business to use for advertisements.[184] Dick Clark, host of popular television shows such as "American Bandstand" and "Dick Clark's Rockin New Year's Eve" gave Olive Enterprises, Inc. ("Olive") the exclusive right to use his name for commercial benefit through a loan agreement.[185] Olive obtained an official service mark for

[183] New Kids on the Block v. News America Pub., Inc., 971 F.2d 302, 308 (9th Cir. 1992).
[184] Clark v. America Online Inc., No. CV-98-5650, 2000 WL 33535712, *1 (C.D. Cal. 2000).
[185] Id.

"Dick Clark" through the USPTO. America Online Inc. ("AOL") began an advertising campaign where they included in their logo: "If you danced to the Beatles, cruised in a Thunderbird, or tuned into Dick Clark, you earned ... 100 hours free [internet service on AOL]."[186] Olive then sued AOL for trademark infringement and AOL raised the defense of nominative fair use.

The first element of the nominative fair use test requires the product or service to not be readily identifiable without use of the trademark. A trademark of an individual's legal name makes it extremely hard to refer to that person without using the trademark. Therefore, the first requirement of nominative fair use is met where there is no *descriptive substitute* for describing the individual and the only option for referring to him is by using his name. In this case, it was deemed unwieldy to refer to Dick Clark as "that personable announcer of that TV dance show from the 1960s." The court found that the first prong of the test was met.[187]

The second element requires that only so much of the mark or marks that are *reasonably necessary* to identify the product or service may be used. In our example, AOL did not put the term "Dick Clark" in larger font than any other term in the advertisement.[188] The argument was made the color combination of Dick Clark's name was more visible

---

[186] *Id.*
[187] *Id.* at 5.
[188] *Id.*

than the other words; but the court found this to be a stretch.[189] Ultimately, the size and font of the mark in the advertisement were only used to refer to the TV personality and no unnecessary tools, such as photographs, were used to identify him. Therefore, the court found AOL's use of the mark was no more than reasonably necessary to identify the TV show host.[190]

The third and final element requires that the user must do nothing to suggest *sponsorship or endorsement* by the trademark holder. There was no indication in AOL's advertisement that suggested joint sponsorship or endorsement from Olive.[191] There were no references made to Olive in the advertisement and it is not practical to believe anyone would make the assumption that Olive was involved with the internet service being offered. Therefore, all three elements for determining nominative fair use were met in this case. This means that AOL's actions were protected by the Lanham Act and there is no trademark infringement.

In contrast, an example where nominative fair use would not be granted is where two publishing companies create book titles with nearly the same title and use the same font to display it.[192] The trademark-owning manufacturer created a book with the title "Oh, the

---

189 *Id.*
190 *Id.*
191 *Id.*
192 Dr. Seuss Enterprises, L.P. v. ComicMix LLC, 300 F.Supp.3d 1073 (S.D. Cal. 2017).

Places You'll Go!" and the junior using manufacturer published a book with the title "Oh, the Places You'll Boldly Go!"[193] In this case, it was deemed the second element of the nominative fair use test was not met because using the identical font, down to the shape and size of the exclamation point, is using more of the trademark than is reasonably necessary to identify the book.[194] It does not matter that the first and third elements of the test were met, because all three need to be met for protection under the nominative fair use defense.

IV.   Classic and Nominative Fair Use

Classic and nominative fair use defenses are entirely separate and distinct defenses to accusations of infringement.

A likelihood of confusion is not a factor when evaluating classic fair use but is a factor for nominative fair use.[195]

Classic fair use is where the language of a trademark is not being used for the purposes of a trademark. Instead, the mark is being used to describe the junior user's product and the use is permissible despite any likelihood of confusion.

---

[193] *Id.* at 1077
[194] *Id.* at 1090; *See also* Toho Co. v. William Morrow and Co., 33 F.Supp.2d 1206, 1211 (C.D. Cal. 1998).
[195] KP Permanent Make-Up, Inc. v. Lasting Impression I, Inc., 328 F.3d 1061, 1072 (9th Cir. 2003); *see also* William Spieler, *Nominative Fair Use in Trademark Law: A Fair Use Like No Other* 89 J. PAT. & TRADEMARK OFF. SOC'Y 780, 786 (2007).

A nominative fair use defense is predicated on a junior user employing the mark because it is associated with the trademark owner's goods.[196] Therefore, the descriptive word is not being used for a descriptive purpose, but rather is used because of its secondary meaning.

The other difference between classic and nominative fair use is the manner in which the trademark is being used. Under classic fair use, the trademark is only being used to describe the product or services being promoted by the junior user. This is different from nominative fair use, in which the trademark is specifically being used for the purpose of the trademark.

The table below summarizes the factors involved in classic versus nominative fair use:

---

[196] *Id.*

	Fair Use Test	Likelihood of Confusion
Classic Fair Use	• Junior user's use of the term is not as a trademark or service mark • Junior user uses the term "fairly and in good faith" • Junior user uses the term only to describe its goods or services	1. Not a factor → does not matter if there is any confusion about trademark owner's involvement
Nominative Fair Use	• The plaintiff's product or service in question must be one not readily identifiable without use of the trademark, • Only so much of the mark or marks may be used as is reasonably necessary to identify the plaintiff's product or service • The user must do nothing that would, in conjunction with the mark, suggest sponsorship or endorsement by the trademark holder	2. Factor → use of the mark cannot cause any confusion about the trademark owner's involvement

CJ's Tip: Keep the above table in mind when you are planning on using another's trademark. As long as you meet all of the criteria, you will likely have the legal right to use the trademark.

CHAPTER 7: NEGATIVE ASSOCIATIONS

I.   Introduction

It is important to protect a trademark from various negative associations with junior users of the mark. The two primary negative associations that this chapter will discuss are:

(1) "assignment in gross" and

(2) "dilution."

An assignment in gross is where a non-owner uses the rights' owner's trademark without a transfer of goodwill. Assignments in gross are not valid and Sellers who own the marks can seek orders from a court directing the non-owner to stop using the mark.

CJ's Tip: When a Court orders someone to do something or to refrain from doing something, it is called "injunctive relief."

Dilution is where a famous trademark has lost its distinctiveness. There are two forms of dilution: (1) tarnishment and (2) blurring.

Tarnishment is where a junior user's employment of a mark hurts the reputation of the mark. This form of dilution is relatively straightforward and easy to prove. The harder, and more common, form of dilution is where a junior user uses a mark in connection with their own good or services, but it is still clear to the consumers that the brands are not associated.

> Anthony's Preview: Negative associations with your trademark are obviously bad for your brand. This chapter will discuss tools to protect your trademark from negative associations.

II.   Assignment in Gross

An assignment of a trademark is when a business or party transfers all of their rights to a trademark they own to another party. A trademark is "assignable with the good will of the business in which the mark is used, or with that part of the good will of the business connected with the use of and symbolized by the mark."[197] "Goodwill" is defined as the benefit received from the assignor beyond the value of the capital, stock, funds, or property, but rather the public perception and loyal customers gained from use of the mark.[198] Courts look at whether any *physical* or *tangible* assets have been transferred to the assignee when determining if goodwill has been transferred.[199] Therefore, evidence that should be used to demonstrate a transfer of goodwill include: (1) customer lists; (2) production plans showing that your client will produce the product that originally carried the mark; and (3) any secret

---

[197] 14 U.S.C. § 1060 (2016); *See also* Glow Industries, Inc. v. Lopez, 273 F.Supp.2d 1095, 1107 (C.D. Cal. 2003).

[198] Newark Morning Ledger Co. v. United States, 507 U.S. 546, 555 (1993) (quoting Metropolitan Bank v. St. Louis Dispatch Co., 149 U.S. 436 (1893)).

[199] *Guide to Records Retention*, 3 Records Retention § 60:11 (last updated May 2018).

formula or other necessary documents the product needs to be manufactured.[200]

> CJ's Side Note: This means that as the assignee, you must sell the same exact product to your customers that the original owner of the trademark produced; otherwise, there would be confusion. For example, if "Apple" agreed to sell you their trademark, you cannot use it to create a business that sells granny smith apples. You would need to continue to sell computers, tablets or other products currently sold by Apple.

However, not all assignments are valid. A "naked" or "in gross" transfer of a mark, which is not transferred with the associated goodwill, is invalid.[201] The purpose of prohibiting the assignment of a trademark in gross is to prevent consumers from being *misled* or *confused* about where the source and quality of the goods or services they are buying.[202]

In the words of a Federal Court, "use of the mark by the assignee in connection with a different goodwill and different product would result in a fraud on the purchasing public who reasonably assume that the mark signifies the same thing, whether used by one person or

---

[200] *Id.*
[201] *Glow Industries, Inc.*, 273 F.Supp.2d at 1107.
[202] Sugar Busters LLC v. Brennan, 177 F.3d 258, 265 (5th Cir. 1999); *see also* Visa, U.S.A., Inc. v. Birmingham Trust Nat'l Bank, 696 F.2d 1371, 1375 (Fed. Cir. 1982).

another."[203] Goodwill is a requirement when assigning a trademark "to maintain the continuity of the product or service symbolized by the mark and thereby avoid deceiving or confusing customers."[204]

An important aspect of trademark assignments is that courts have upheld assignments where the assignee's product or service is

"substantially similar" to that of the assignor and would not confuse customers.[205] For example, a mark that represents a promise to pay a check can be assigned from a supermarket chain to a credit card company.[206] This allows a trademark to be transferred without actually transferring any tangible assets. The assignee only needs to produce a product that is of the same *quality* and *nature* of the product previously produced under the trademark.[207]

---

[203] Marshak v. Green, 746 F.2d 927, 929 (2d Cir. 1984).
[204] E. & J. Gallo Winery v. Gallo Cattle Co., 967 F.2d 1280, 1289 (9th Cir. 1992) (citing J. THOMAS MCCARTHY, 1 MCCARTHY ON TRADEMARKS AND UNFAIR COMPETITION § 18:1(c)).
[205] *Marshak*, 746 F.2d at 930.
[206] *Visa, U.S.A., Inc.*, 696 F.2d 1371.
[207] Clark & Freeman Corp. v. Heartland Co. Ltd., 811 F.Supp. 137 (S.D.N.Y. 1993) (quoting Defiance Button Machine Co. v. C&C Metal Products Corp., 759 F.2d 1053, 1059 (2d Cir. 1985)).

There is no universal test to determine "substantial similarity." The facts for each case are unique. The existence or lack of substantial similarity is determined on a case-by-case basis.

One Court held there to be substantial similarity between an assignor who sold "all-weather coats and women's coats" and an assignee who sells "various items of clothing including jackets, rain wear and various items of apparel" under the same trademark.[208] The Court reasoned that the two companies had substantially similar characteristics by both selling apparel primarily to women. However, not all cases with small differences are covered under the umbrella of substantial similarity. Another Court determined a case where the assignor's cola-flavored syrup and an assignee's pepper-flavored syrup were different enough and, therefore did not cause confusion amongst consumers.[209]

III.   Dilution

Dilution is the diminishment of a distinctive trademark's ability to identify the goods and services associated with it, even where the average consumer would not think the junior and senior users were related or connected.[210] Dilution focuses on the protection of the trademark asset to the trademark owner, rather than the confusion

---

[208] Main Street Outfitters v. Federated Dep't Stores, 730 F.Supp. 289 (D.Minn. 1989).
[209] PepsiCo, Inc. v. Grapette Co., 416 F.2d 285 (8th Cir. 1969).
[210] Lynda J. Oswald, *"Tarnishment" and "Blurring" Under the Federal Trademark Dilution Act of 1995*, 36 AM. BUS. L.J. 255, 260 (1999).

caused for the consumer. "The goal of dilution theory is to eliminate any 'risk of an erosion of the public's identification of [a] very strong mark with the plaintiff alone' and to prevent another user from 'diminishing [a mark's] distinctiveness, uniqueness, effectiveness, and prestigious connotations.'"[211]

An example of an analysis of dilution occurred where a determination of whether a company known as "Kodak Piano" would dilute the Kodak mark owned by the photography company, Eastman Kodak Company.[212]

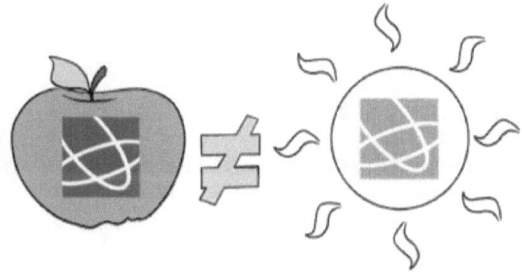

The Dilution Act of 1995 changed several key concepts associated with trademark law. Before the Act, the Lanham Act only protected marks where there was a likelihood of confusion. The goal of the Dilution Act was to broaden the federal protection of trademarks, particularly because many marks are used nationally and internationally. Most importantly, the Act creates a property-like right

[211] Elvis Presley Enters, Inc. v. Capece, 950 F.Supp. 783, 797 (S.D. Tex. 1996) (quoting Tiffany & Co. v. Boston Club, Inc., 231 F.Supp. 836, 844 (D.Mass. 1964).
[212] Oswald, *supra* note 210, at 260-61.

on the trademark to protect against any diminishing use of the mark in the marketplace.[213]

> CJ's Tip: You cannot use another's trademark just because you sell a completely different product or service. Just because there is no likelihood of confusion does not mean the trademark owner has other rights to protect their mark.

Dilution protects a trademark's "selling power." Dilution primarily applies to distinctive or famous marks, since weak marks have no selling power.[214]

The best way to determine whether a mark has "selling power" is by evaluating whether the mark has acquired "secondary meaning."

A leading legal treatise, The Restatement (Third) of Unfair Competition, states "a trademark is sufficiently distinctive to be diluted by a non-confusing use if the mark retains its source significance when encountered outside the context of the goods or services with which the mark is used by the trademark owner."[215]

---

[213] *Id.* at 261.
[214] *Id.*
[215] McCARTHY, *supra* note 204, § 25 cmt. e (1995).

The Dilution Act lists eight non-exclusive factors for a court to consider when determining whether a mark is distinctive or famous: (1) the degree of inherent or acquired distinctiveness of the mark; (2) the duration and extent of use of the mark in connection with the goods or services with which the mark is used; (3) the duration and extent of advertising and publicity of the mark; (4) the geographical extent of the trading area in which the mark is used; (5) the channels of trade for the goods or services with which the mark is used;(6) the degree of recognition for the mark in the trading areas and channels of trade used by the mark's owner and the person against whom the injunction is sought; (7) the nature and extent of use of the same or similar marks by third parties; and (8) whether the mark was registered under federal law.[216] While these factors give courts guidance, determining whether a trademark is "famous" is always specific to the facts of a particular case.

A. Tarnishment:

Tarnishment is a form of dilution where a junior user's use of a mark or similar mark hurts the reputation of the mark.

The Trademark Dilution Revision Act ("TDRA") of 2006 defines tarnishment as an "association arising from the similarity

---

[216] 15 U.S.C. § 1125(c)(1) (Supp. II 1996).

between a mark or trade name and a famous mark that harms the reputation of the famous mark."[217]

Establishing dilution by tarnishment requires:

    (1) at least one of their asserted trademarks was valid and distinctive prior to the junior user's use of the mark;

    (2) there is similarity between the junior user's mark and the trademark owner's mark; and

    (3) the accused use will likely cause negative associations that damage the reputation of the famous mark.[218]

The trademark dilution by tarnishment test was applied where a toy company produced a line of dog toys that were based off famous alcoholic beverage companies.[219] One of the toys developed was the "Bad Spaniel," a play on the famous Jack Daniels whiskey bottle. The Court determined that Jack Daniel's trademark was famous at the time of the junior user's use where the general consuming public would widely recognize it. In this instance, it was found that the Jack Daniels trademark was famous because it had been used consistently for over a century, it is prominently featured on their website that is visited over 4 million times a year, and it is prominently featured on the social media

---

[217] 15 U.S.C. § 1125(c)(2)(C); *See also* Mattel, Inc. v. MCA Records, Inc., 296 F.3d 894, 903 (9th Cir. 2002).
[218] 15 U.S.C. §1225(c); *See also* VIP Products, LLC v. Jack Daniel's Properties, Inc., 219 F.Supp.3d 891, 900 (D. Ariz. 2018).
[219] *VIP Products, LLC*, 219 F.Supp.3d at 899.

pages.[220] The marks were similar because the toy company designed the "Bad Spaniels" toy to be identical to a Jack Daniels whiskey bottle; the toy had the same square shape bottle, ribbed neck, arched letter, filigreed border, black and white color scheme, fonts, shapes, styles, and the products were identical size.[221] Finally, the toy company's use of the trademark created a bad reputation for the Jack Daniels brand because Jack Daniels whiskey is sold for human consumption, which does not mix with the references to canine excrement made on the "Bad Spaniel" toy.[222]

B. Blurring:

The harder form of dilution for sellers to prove is "blurring." Blurring exists where a famous mark or similar mark is used in connection with the goods or services of a junior user.[223] When this occurs, the trademark owner fears that consumers will no longer associate the mark *exclusively* with their goods or services. Courts established six factors to evaluate accusations of blurring:

    (1) similarity of the marks;

    (2) similarity of the products covered by the marks;

    (3) sophistication of plaintiff's customers;

---

[220] *Id.* at 900-01.
[221] *Id.* at 901.
[222] *Id.* at 904. (Referencing the "Bad Spaniels" toy, which reads "43% POO BY VOL" and "100% SMELLY.")
[223] Oswald, *supra* note 210, at 262-3.

(4) predatory intent of defendant;

(5) renown of the senior mark; and

(6) renown of the junior mark.[224]

When determining similarity of the marks, the junior mark does not need to be identical to the senior mark. For example, a Court found that a travel department using the promotion "The Greatest Snow on Earth" did not need to be identical to the senior mark "The Greatest Show on Earth" to be evaluated for blurring.[225] So long as the implication of the marks are the same, a court will find substantial similarity between the marks.[226]

> Anthony's Breakdown: The Dilution Act, along with the component of similarity of products, make dilution cases no longer exclusive to noncompeting companies. This means, even if you are in the same market and the consumers would not be confused as to the difference between you and the junior user, you could still preclude junior user's use of your mark through a blurring action.

---

[224] *Id.* at 285.
[225] Ringling Brothers-Barnum & Bailey, Combined Shows, Inc. v. Utah Div. of Travel Department, 935 F.Supp. 763, 765 (E.D. Va. 1996).
[226] Oswald, *supra* note 210, at 288. *See also* American Exp. Co. v. CFK, Inc., 947 F.Supp. 310, 317 (E.D. Mich. 1996).

Courts take the sophistication of the consumer into consideration when making decisions. The concept is the more sophisticated the Sellers' customers are, the less likely they are to make a mistake about the association between the junior user and senior user's mark. For example, the higher sophistication of credit card customers makes blurring less likely than customers at a convenience store.[227]

The next factor is whether the junior user had the predatory intent of benefitting commercially from association with the senior mark. Intent increases the likelihood of blurring; absence of intent will *not* relieve the junior user of blurring.[228] Predatory intent is a major factor in determining remedies where blurring is found.

The fifth factor is the renown, or fame, of the senior mark. The more famous the trademark, the more likely a court will protect it from blurring. A senior mark that is not famous can still be diluted through blurring, but a nationally recognized mark will not need to focus as much on the other factors in this test.[229] If the senior mark is not nationally famous, the court will force them to prove substantial similarity, product similarity, or sophistication of customers to a greater extent.

---

[227] *American Express Co.*, 947 F.Supp. at 318; *See also* Wawa, Inc. v. Haaf, 40 U.S.P.Q.2d (BNA) 1629, 1629 (E.D. Pa. 1996).
[228] Oswald, *supra* note 210, at 292.
[229] *Id.* at 293.

The final factor needed to evaluate to establish blurring is the renown of the junior mark. The important distinction to make here is whether the product or service of the junior user is new to the market or has been established.[230] If the junior user is new to the market, blurring will likely not be found. However, where the junior user has used the mark for a significant period of time and established some fame, blurring may be found. This factor often leads courts to discount blurring because: (1) if the junior mark is not renowned at first, it could become more renowned over time through marketing and other tactics and (2) the effect of one junior mark may be minor, but the effect of allowing several junior marks could impede business and dilute the senior mark.[231]

The following identifies potential remedies and defenses to dilution:

---

[230] *Id.* at 294.
[231] *Id.* at 295.

Remedies for Dilution	Defenses to Dilution
• Injunction against the junior user's commercial use of the mark • If you can prove the junior user acted with intent → expands remedies to profits made, actual damages, attorney fees, and an order requiring destruction of the offending items	• Ownership of a valid registration under prior trademark acts or on the Principal Register • Fair use of the mark in comparative advertising • Noncommercial use of the mark • All forms of the news reporting and commentary

CHAPTER 8 – PROTECTING YOUR TRADEMARK
ON AND OFFLINE

I.   Introduction

This last and final chapter will serve as a rudimentary overview of how a seller can best police his or her brand and ensure that any infringement which occurs can be reliably and timely caught. This chapter is a primer on the process, costs, and possible rewards of pursuing a lawsuit against an infringer.

II.   Vigilant Policing of Your Mark

There are many ways Sellers can monitor their brands and marks.

A simple method of monitoring marks is via Google.[232]   Google Alerts is a free service which provides automated monitoring of results that match or fall within parameters specified by the user.[233]   Google sends Alerts to the user's inbox every time these results are picked up by Google at whatever frequency the user dictates.[234]   As of the publishing of this book, Google does not send alerts from social media or from web sites or pages on the web that Google does not index.[235] However, the ease with which Google Alerts and the lack of any cost makes Google Alerts a good place for smaller brands to start their brand monitoring.

Google Alerts can be set up and activated at www.google.com/alerts and then by typing in whatever term the user desires to have a notification sent to them regarding.[236] A carwash solution Seller that obtained a mark for "Red Banana," for example, might want to specify that Google send an Alerts regarding "red banana," "red banana carwash," "yellow banana carwash," or "banana car soap."

---

[232] *Trademark 101: Monitoring Strategies You Can Implement,* SECUREYOURTRADEMARK.COM (last visited July 10, 2018), https://secureyourtrademark.com/blog/trademark-101-monitoring-strategies-can-implement.

[233] Patrick Whatman, *How to Set Up Google Alerts and Go Even Further,* MENTION (last viewed July 10, 2018), https://mention.com/blog/how-to-set-up-google-alerts.

[234] *Id.*

[235] *Id.*

[236] Jerri Collins, *Google Alerts: What They Are, How to Make One,* LIFEWIRE (May 7, 2018), https://www.lifewire.com/google-alerts-3481816.

After defining the search parameters, the Seller selects "Show Options" to tailor the Alerts to his or her preferences.[237] The Seller can specify the frequency of the notifications, the language in which these notifications should be, the types of websites which should be included (e.g. Amazon, Etsy, other internet retailers), regions within which the search results originate, and the email address where notifications should be sent.[238]

Sellers concerned about trademark infringers may also routinely examine the Gazette. The Gazette is the printed collection of all published, renewed, and cancelled trademark applications.[239] Published every Tuesday. The Gazette is available in an electronic format and is completely free.[240] Routine monthly checks of the Gazette will help Sellers who own marks stay abreast of possible infringers. The Gazette is the same publication USPTO Examiners consult before approving a trademark and in which an application will be published for a full 30 days before full registration. The Gazette has a significant number of marks in each issue…sometimes in excess of 16,000 marks.

The USPTO also has a searchable database. The Trademark Electronic Search System ("TESS") will return a list of results

---

[237] *Id.*
[238] *Id.*
[239] *Trademark Official Gazette*, USPTO (last visited July 10, 2018), https://www.uspto.gov/learning-and-resources/official-gazette/trademark-official-gazette-tmog.
[240] *Id.*

comprising of all trademarks or trademark applications known to the USPTO as relating to the search query.[241] Used in conjunction with Google Alerts, TESS offers an instantaneous review of all USPTO-known trademarks or trademark applications and expands the search for infringing marks beyond Google.[242]

Searching for trademarks on the TESS is simple and straight forward. A quick Google search of the term "TESS" will return, as the first result, a link to the database itself, which is offered free of charge and requires no membership or email address to use. From there, one must select one of three search options: a "Basic Word Mark Search" is useful for focusing solely on wordmarks; the "Word and/or Design Mark Search (Structured)" can be used for searching both word and design mark (i.e. trade dress); and the "Word and/or Design Mark Search (Free Form)" is similar to the previous option in that it allows one to search for both word and design marks, but with the added ability to use Boolean search terms to expand the results.[243] If utilized on a routine basis, TESS checks may prove essential to guarding against trademark infringement.

---

[241] *Id.*
[242] *Id.*
[243] Trademark Electronic Search System (TESS), USPTO (last visited July 10, 2018), http://tmsearch.uspto.gov/bin/gate.exe?f=tess&state=4809:3n12zy.1.1.

III.   The Legal Process

If a trademark infringer is detected, what can be done? The answer depends on the platform the Seller is operating on, as well as in what specific ways the trademark was infringed upon.

Anthony's Advice: It should be stressed again that, after you detect the presence of trademark infringement, it is imperative that you retain the services of a practiced trademark attorney. Navigating the waters of the legal process is treacherous without the proper knowledge of how to avoid its associated pitfalls and quagmires.

After determining the nature of the infringement, the Seller, through his or her attorney, will generally send a "Cease and Desist" letter. A Cease and Desist letter requests that the infringer refrain from further violating intellectual property rights. Generally, the letter notifies the infringer that if the offending products, bearing the infringing mark, are not removed from the view of consumers, further legal or other action may follow.

If the Seller is an Amazon merchant who has fallen victim to infringement at the hands of another Amazon merchant, the Seller's attorney may file a takedown request with Amazon. This takedown request will be considered by Amazon and may be either granted.

When Amazon complies with the takedown request, infringers will often resume selling the infringing product under a different Amazon account.

If financially feasible, Sellers who suffer infringement can seek redress in court.

IV.   Outcomes

When a court has determined that trademark infringement has occurred: (1) a seller could be awarded monetary damages or (2) a seller could be awarded injunctive relief. An injunction is far more common for trademark infringement cases since it is hard to equate the amount

of monetary loss incurred on a seller due to the infringement.

Damages awarded for a trademark infringement action include all injuries and loss of profits to a seller's business that are *proximately* caused by the infringer's actions.[244] The seller only needs to prove they suffered actual harm as a result of the infringement; they do not need to prove the exact amount of damages they suffered. The court has the power to assess the actual damages under their own discretion based on the circumstances of the case.[245] If the damages are burdensome or unavailable, the court will award what they find just, whether it be monetary or injunctive relief.

The Lanham Act allows sellers to recover lost profits or any damages from trademark infringement. The Act lists five types of monetary relief for trademark owners to compensate infringement: (1) an accounting of an infringer's profits; (2) the actual damages the trademark owner sustained; (3) a reasonable royalty representing a measure of the trademark owner's damages; (4) attorney's fees in exceptional cases; and (5) costs.[246] There is a special monetary remedy for cases involving counterfeit goods, where the court awards treble damages, a variant of damages which triple the amount of actual or compensatory damages, or profits earned from sale of the counterfeit goods, whichever is higher.[247] However, prevailing in a trademark infringement case does not guarantee monetary relief for a seller. Monetary damages are generally rare, and injunctions are the most

---

[244] Griffith, *supra* note 68, § 367.
[245] *Id.*
[246] 15 U.S.C. § 1117(a) (2016).
[247] 15 U.S.C. § 1117(b).

common form of relief for Lanham Act cases.[248] In order to be awarded monetary damages, the Seller must prove there was customer confusion that caused economic loss or that the infringer was unjustly enriched.

Customer confusion is established via either (1) evidence of diversion of sales or (2) by presenting survey results showing actual customer confusion with the mark's owner.[249]

For example, a football helmet manufacturer was denied monetary damages from infringement on a mount that connects the face mask to the helmet. The Court determined this because the manufacturing company did not submit any affidavits or evidence to established customer confusion.[250]

CJ's Side Note: It is important to not rely on being awarded monetary damages when seeking action against trademark infringers. Statistics show only 5.5% of all Lanham Act cases decided between 1947 and 2005 obtained any damages at all.[251] This is because it can be hard to prove consumer confusion and to make the connection between that confusion and economic loss for your company. Injunctions are far more common and a

---

[248] Kenneth L. Port, *Trademark Extortion: The End of Trademark Law*, 65 WASH. & LEE. L REV., 585, 622 (2008).
[249] Schutt Mfg. Co. v. Riddell, Inc., 673 F.2d 202, 206-07 (7th Cir. 1982).
[250] *Id.* at 207.
[251] Port, *supra* note 248, at 622.

more realistic goal when taking action against trademark infringers.

A preliminary injunction is granted to keep an infringer from continuing to infringe on someone's trademark while the case in ongoing. Under the Lanham Act, a Seller seeking a preliminary injunction must establish: (1) the Seller is likely to suffer irreparable harm in absence of preliminary relief; (2) the Seller is likely to succeed on the merits; (3) the seller is likely to suffer irreparable harm in absence of preliminary relief; (4) the injunction is in public interest; and (5) that the balance of equities tips in the Seller's favor.[252] A preliminary injunction will not be granted unless the Seller clearly establishes all of these elements. When deciding whether to grant a preliminary injunction, the court will consider the type of injury the Seller would suffer without one. Please see the following chart detailing how to meet the elements for getting a preliminary injunction:

---

[252] Griffith, *supra* note 68, § 335; *see also* Peoples Federal Sav. Bank v. People's United Bank, 672 F.3d 1 (1st Cir. 2012); Pom Wonderful LLC v. Hubbard, 775 F.3d 1118 (9th Cir. 2014); Derma Pen, LLC v. 4EverYoung Ltc., 773 F.3d 1117 (10th Cir. 2014); Express Franchise Services, L.P. v. Impact Outsourcing Solutions Inc., 244 F.Supp.3d 1368 (N.D. Ga. 2017).

Prerequisite for *Preliminary Injunction*	Defined
Irreparable Harm	Where there is likely irreparable harm to the Seller in the absence of an injunction, rather than merely irreparable injury, and that the harm is imminent.
Likelihood of Success	If the seller establishes that he has a *better than negligible* chance of succeeding on the merits on the underlying infringement claim.
Public Interest	Must determine: (1) the public's interest in not being confused; (2) the public's interest in encouraging competition; and (3) the broader implications of a preliminary injunction.
Balance of Equities	The balance favors an injunction where the irreparable harm to the seller outweighs the monetary cost to the infringer.

<u>Anthony's Breakdown:</u> A preliminary injunction will not be granted if (1) the infringer has discontinued their use of the mark and does not intend to resume use at any point or (2) if the Seller laches or delays bringing action after becoming aware of the infringer's use.[253] Therefore, make sure you bring action quickly after learning of an infringer's use of your mark.

When determining whether to grant a permanent injunction, the Court must determine whether equitable relief is appropriate.[254] The Lanham Act allows for a permanent injunction where: (1) the seller has or will suffer an irreparable injury; (2) remedies at law, such as monetary damages, are inadequate to compensate the injury; (3) a remedy in equity is warranted because of the balance of the hardships between the seller and the infringer; and (4) the public interest would not be harmed if a permanent injunction was granted.[255]

---

[253] Griffith, *supra* note 68, § 345.
[254] La Quinta Worldwide LLC v. Q.R.T.M., S.A. de C.V., 762 F.3d 867, 880 (9th Cir. 2014).
[255] Griffith, *supra* note 68, § 346.

Prerequisite for *Permanent Injunction*	Defined
Irreparable Harm	Where a seller has established he has suffered irreparable injury. An irreparable injury is established where an ordinary purchaser would be confused about the source of the goods or services.
Inadequate Remedies at Law	It is generally recognized that where irreparable harm has been found, there are no adequate remedies at law.
Balance of Hardships	The Court will look for a balance that weighs strongly in favor of issuing a permanent injunction. Generally, an issuing of a preliminary injunction suffices.
Public Interest Served	The public has the right to not be deceived of confused to the owner of a trademark. If the Court finds confusion exists, the public interest would be served through an injunction.

V.   Conclusion

A trademark is an extremely important and necessary tool for protecting Sellers' brands. An important for Sellers developing their brand is registering their trademark. Without registering their trademarks, Sellers are susceptible to economic loss due other Seller infringing on their mark and manipulating market confusion and costing Sellers money.

TABLE OF AUTHORITIES

- *Guide to Records Retention* 3 Records Retention § 60:11 (last updated May 2018).
- 14 U.S.C. § 1060 (2016).
- 15 U.S.C. § 1052 (2016).
- 15 U.S.C. § 1064 (2016).
- 15 U.S.C. § 1117 (2016).
- 15 U.S.C. § 1125 (2016).
- 15 U.S.C. § 1127 (2016).
- Abercrombie & Fitch Co. v. Hunting World, Inc., 537 F.2d 4 (1976).
- *About Trademark Infringement*, U.S.P.T.O. (last visited July 16, 2018), https://www.uspto.gov/page/about-trademark-infringement.
- Adidas-Salomon AG v. Target Corp., 228 F.Supp.2d 1192 (D. Or. 2002).
- Allergan, Inc. v. KRL Group, Inc., 2013 WL 5946235 (T.T.A.B. 2013).
- American Exp. Co. v. CFK, Inc., 947 F.Supp. 310 (E.D. Mich. 1996).
- Anne Gilson LaLonde, *Proving Ownership Online ... and Keeping It: The Internet's Impact on Trademark Use and Coexistence*, 104 TRADEMARK REP. 1275 (2014).
- Aromatique, Inc. v. Gold Seal, Inc., 28 F.3d 863 (8th Cir. 1994).

- Arthur L. Plevy, *How to Obtain Patents, Trademarks and Copyrights*, 161-JUN N.J. LAW. 12 (1994).

- Barbara's Bakery, Inc. v. Barbara Landesman, 2007 WL 196406 (T.T.A.B. 2007).

- Bayer Co. v. United Drug Co., 272 F. 505 (S.D.N.Y. 1921).

- Beverly W. Pattishall, *The Lanham Trademark Act at Fifty – Some History and Comment*, 86 TRADEMARK REP. 442 (1996).

- BREND A. OLSON, 20B2 MINN. PRAC., BUS. REG. IN MINNESOTA – FEDERAL § 2.160 (2018 ed.)

- Brian L. Berlandi, *What State am I in?: Common Law Trademarks on the Internet* 4 MICH. TELECOMM. & TECH. L. REV. 105 (1999).

- Cairns v. Franklin Mint Co., 292 F.3d 1139 (9th Cir. 2002).

- Champagne Louis Roederer v. Delicato Vineyards, 148 F.3d 1373 (Fed. Cir. 1998)

- Citigroup Inc. v. Capital City Bank Group, Inc., 637 F.3d 1344 (Fed. Cir. 2011).

- Clark v. America Online Inc., No. CV-98-5650, 2000 WL 33535712 (C.D. Cal. 2000).

- Clark & Freeman Corp. v. Heartland Co. Ltd., 811 F.Supp. 137 (S.D.N.Y. 1993).

- Dan Nosowitz, *Häagen-Dazs Ice Cream Is From the Bronx— So What's With the Name?*, ATLAS OBSUCRA (Sept. 5, 2017), https://www.atlasobscura.com/articles/haagen-dazs-fake-foreign-branding.

- Daniel Zendel & Dennis Prahl, *Making Sense of Trademarks: Colors, Sounds, & Scents*, LADAS & PARRY (Feb. 16, 1996), https://ladas.com/education-center/making-sense-trademarks-colors-sounds-scents.

- David Johnson, *Trademarks: A History*, INFOPLEASE, https://www.infoplease.com/trademarks-history.

- Defiance Button Machine Co. v. C&C Metal Products Corp., 759 F.2d 1053 (2d Cir. 1985).

- Derma Pen, LLC v. 4EverYoung Ltc., 773 F.3d 1117 (10th Cir. 2014).

- Dr. Seuss Enterprises, L.P. v. ComicMix LLC, 300 F.Supp.3d 1073 (S.D. Cal. 2017).

- E. & J. Gallo Winery v. Gallo Cattle Co., 967 F.2d 1280 (9th Cir. 1992).

- Elvis Presley Enters, Inc. v. Capece, 950 F.Supp. 783 (S.D. Tex. 1996).

- Entrepreneur Media, Inc. v. Smith, 279 F.2d 1135 (9th Cir. 2002).

- Express Franchise Services, L.P. v. Impact Outsourcing Solutions Inc., 244 F.Supp.3d 1368 (N.D. Ga. 2017).

- Fuddruckers, Inc. v. Doc's B.R. Others, Inc., 826 F.2d 837 (9th Cir. 1987).

- Glow Industries, Inc. v. Lopez, 273 F.Supp.2d 1095 (C.D. Cal. 2003).

- *History of Trademarks: Everything You Need to Know*, UPCOUNSEL, https://www.upcounsel.com/history-of-trademarks.

- *How Long Does Trademark Protection Last*, REGISTERINGATRADEMARK.COM (last visited July 16, 2018), http://www.registeringatrademark.com/length-trademark.shtml.

- *Individual Fees Under the Madrid Protocol*, WIPO (last updated June 2, 2018), http://www.wipo.int/madrid/en/fees/ind_taxes.html.

- *In re* Becton, Dickinson and Co., 675 F.3d 1368 (2012).

- *In re* Chevron Intellectual Prop. Grp. LLC, 96 U.S.P.Q.2d 2026 (TTAB 2010).

- *In re* Chippendales USA, Inc., 622 F.3d 1346 (Fed. Cir. 2010).

- *In re* Clarke, 17 U.S.P.Q.2d 1238 (T.T.A.B. 1990).

- *In re* E.I. Du Pont de Nemours & Co., 476 F.2d 1357 (C.C.P.A. 1973).

- *In re* General Electric Broadcasting Company, Inc., 199 U.S.P.Q. 560 (T.T.A.B. 1978).

- *In re* Majestic Distilling Co., 315 F.3d 1311 (Fed.Cir.2003).

- *In re* MDG Tools, Inc., 2010 TTAB LEXIS 230 (T.T.A.B. 2010).

- *In re* Mighty Leaf Tea, 601 F.3d 1342 (Fed. Cir. 2010).

- *In re* Owens-Corning Fiberglas Corp., 774 F.2d 1116 (Fed. Cir. 1985).

- *In re* SL&E Training Stable, Inc., 2008 WL 4107225 (T.T.A.B. 2008).

- International Order of Job's Daughters v. Lindeburg & Co., 633 F.2d 912 (9th Cir. 1980), cert. denied, 452 U.S. 941 (1981).

- Inwood Labs., Inc. v. Ives Labs., Inc., 456 U.S. 844 (1982).

- JAMES E. HAWES & AMANDA V. DWIGHT, 1 TRADEMARK REGISTRATION PRAC. § 3:1 (2018 ed.).

- Jeffrey Milstein, Inc. v. Greger, Lawlor, Roth, Inc., 58, F.3d 27 (2d Cir. 1995).

- Jeff Pietsch, *Trademark Infringement: Factors Considered in Consumer Confusion*, THE IP LAW BLOG (May 9, 2007), https://www.theiplawblog.com/2007/05/articles/trademark-law/trademark-infringement-factors-considered-in-consumer-confusion.

- Joel W. Reese, *Defining the Elements of Trade Dress Infringement Under Section 43(a) of the Lanham Act*, 2 TEX. INTELL. PROP. L.J. 103 (1994).

- John Dwight Ingram, *The Genericide of Trademarks*, 2 BUFF. INTELL. PROP. L.J. 154 (2004).

- John H. Harland Co. v. Clarke Checks, Inc., 711 F.2d 966 (11th Cir. 1983).

- J. THOMAS MCCARTHY, 4 MCCARTHY ON TRADEMARKS AND UNFAIR COMPETITION § 24:43 (5th ed.) (2018).

- Keebler Co. v. Murray Bakery Prods., 866 F.2d 1386 (Fed. Cir. 1989).

- Kelley Keller, *3 Biggest Differences Between the Principal Register and Supplemental Register for Trademarks*, KELLEY KELLER ESQ. (Feb. 2, 2018), http://kelleykeller.com/3-biggest-differences-principal-register-supplemental-register-trademarks.

- Kellogg Co. v. Pack'em Enters., 951 F.2d 330 (Fed.Cir.1991).

- Kendall–Jackson Winery, Limited v. E. & J. Gallo Winery, 150 F.3d 1042 (9th Cir. 1998).

- Kenner Parker Toys Inc. v. Rose Art Industries, Inc., 963 F.2d 350 (Fed. Cir. 1992).

- Kenneth L. Port, *Trademark Extortion: The End of Trademark Law*, 65 WASH. & LEE. L REV., 585 (2008).

- KP Permanent Make-Up, Inc. v. Lasting Impression I, Inc., 328 F.3d 1061 (9th Cir. 2003).

- Landscape Forms, Inc. v. Columbia Cascade Co., 113 F.3d 373 (2d Cir. 1997).

- La Quinta Worldwide LLC v. Q.R.T.M., S.A. de C.V., 762 F.3d 867 (9th Cir. 2014).

- Lonnie E. Griffith et. al., 87 C.J.S. TRADEMARKS, ETC. (2018).

- Lynda J. Oswald, *"Tarnishment" and "Blurring" Under the Federal Trademark Dilution Act of 1995*, 36 AM. BUS. L.J. 255 (1999).

- *Madrid – The International Trademark System*, WIPO (last visited July 16, 2018), http://www.wipo.int/madrid/en.

- Main Street Outfitters v. Federated Dep't Stores, 730 F.Supp. 289 (D.Minn. 1989).

- Marshak v. Green, 746 F.2d 927 (2d Cir. 1984).

- Mattel, Inc. v. MCA Records, Inc., 296 F.3d 894 (9th Cir. 2002).

- Matthew D. Asbell, *Inherent and Acquired Distinctiveness and The Principal and Supplemental Registers for U.S. Trademarks*, LADAS & PARRY (May 1, 2014), https://ladas.com/education-center/inherent-acquired-distinctiveness-principal-supplemental-registers-u-s-trademarks.

- Metropolitan Bank v. St. Louis Dispatch Co., 149 U.S. 436 (1893).

- Michael J. Allen, *The Role of Actual Confusion Evidence in Trademark Infringement Litigation*, 83 TRADEMARK REP. 267 (1993).

- Michael Zhang, *Origin and Evolution of Kodak's Name and Logo*, PETA PIXEL (Aug. 3, 2011), https://petapixel.com/2011/08/03/origin-and-evolution-of-kodaks-name-and-logo.

- Michelle L. Evans, 99 AM. JUR. PROOF OF FACTS 3d 107 *Establishing the Zone of Expansion for Trademark Purposes* § 18 (2018).

- Nautilus Group, Inc. v. Icon Health and Fitness, Inc., 372 F.3d 1330 (Fed. Cir. 2004).

- Newark Morning Ledger Co. v. United States, 507 U.S. 546 (1993).

- New Kids on the Block v. News America Pub., Inc., 971 F.2d 302 (9th Cir. 1992).

- Octocom Systems, Inc. v. Houston Computer Services, Inc., 918 F.2d 937 (Fed. Cir. 1990).

- Odom's Tenn. Pride Sausage, Inc. v. FF Acquisition, L.L.C., 600 F.3d 1343 (Fed. Cir. 2010)

- Paddington Corp. v. Attic Importers & Distributors, Inc., 996 F.2d 577 (1993).

- Patrick Whatman, *How to Set Up Google Alerts and Go Even Further*, MENTION (last viewed July 10, 2018), https://mention.com/blog/how-to-set-up-google-alerts.

- Peoples Federal Sav. Bank v. People's United Bank, 672 F.3d 1 (1st Cir. 2012)

- PepsiCo, Inc. v. Grapette Co., 416 F.2d 285 (8th Cir. 1969).

- Pom Wonderful LLC v. Hubbard, 775 F.3d 1118 (9th Cir. 2014).

- Practical Law Intellectual Property & Technology, *Trade Dress Protection*, THOMSON REUTERS (2018).

- Qualitex Co. v. Jacobson Products Co., Inc., 514 U.S. 159 (1995).

- Ralston Purina Co. v. Thomas J. Lipton, Inc., 341 F. Supp. 129 (S.D.N.Y. 1972).

- Ringling Brothers-Barnum & Bailey, Combined Shows, Inc. v. Utah Div. of Travel Department, 935 F.Supp. 763 (E.D. Va. 1996).

- San Fernando Elec. Mfg. Co. v. JFD Elecs. Components Corp., 565 F.2d 683 (C.C.P.A. 1977).

- Schutt Mfg. Co. v. Riddell, Inc., 673 F.2d 202 (7th Cir. 1982).

- Seabrook Foods, Inc. v. Bar-Well Foods Limited, 568 F.2d 1342 (1977).

- *Second Quarter FY 2018, At a Glance* (last visited July 16, 2018), USPTO, https://www.uspto.gov/dashboards/trademarks/main.dashxml.

- Sega Enterprises Ltd. v. Accolade, Inc., 977 F.2d 1510 (1992).

- Snap-On Tools Co. v. C/Net, Inc., 1997 U.S. Dist. LEXIS 14581 (N.D. Ill. 1997).

- Specialized Seating, Inc. v. Greenwich Industries, LP, 616 F.3d 722 (2010).

- Specialty Brands v. Coffee Bean Distribs., 748 F.2d 669 (Fed. Cir. 1984)

- Squirtco v. Tomy Corp., 697 F.2d 1038 (Fed. Cir. 1983)

- Standard Terry Mills, Inc. v. Shen Mfg. Co., 803 F.2d 778 (3d Cir. 1986).

- Stephanie M. Greene, *Sorting Out "Fair Use" and "Likelihood of Confusion" in Trademark Law*, 43 AM. BUS. L.J. 43 (2006).

- Sugar Busters LLC v. Brennan, 177 F.3d 258 (5th Cir. 1999)

- Sunmark, Inc. v. Ocean Spray Cranberries, Inc., 64 F.3d 1055 (7th Cir. 1995).

- THOMAS D. SELZ et al., ENTERTAINMENT LAW 3D: LEGAL CONCEPTS AND BUSINESS PRACTICES § 17:83 (last updated Dec. 2017).

- Tiffany & Co. v. Boston Club, Inc., 231 F.SUpp. 836 (D.Mass. 1964).

- Tiffany Valeriano, *7 Factors for Identifying Trademark Likelihood of Confusion*, TRADEMARKNOW (Mar. 28, 2017), https://www.trademarknow.com/blog/7-factors-for-identifying-trademark-likelihood-of-confusion.

- Toho Co. v. William Morrow and Co., 33 F.Supp.2d 1206 (C.D. Cal. 1998).

- *Trademark 101: Monitoring Strategies You Can Implement*, SECUREYOURTRADEMARK.COM (last visited July 10, 2018), https://secureyourtrademark.com/blog/trademark-101-monitoring-strategies-can-implement.

- *Trademark Applications – Intent-to-Use (ITU) Basis*, USPTO (last visited July 16, 2018), https://www.uspto.gov/trademarks-application-process/filing-online/intent-use-itu-applications.

- Trademark Electronic Search System (TESS), USPTO (last visited July 10, 2018), http://tmsearch.uspto.gov/bin/gate.exe?f=tess&state=4809:3n1 2zy.1.1.

- *Trademark Official Gazette*, USPTO (last visited July 10, 2018), https://www.uspto.gov/learning-and-resources/official-gazette/trademark-official-gazette-tmog.

- *Trademark: "Sound Mark" Examples*, U.S.P.T.O. (last visited June 16, 2018), https://www.uspto.gov/trademark/soundmarks/trademark-sound-mark-examples

- *Trademarks – What Happens Next?*, USPTO (last visited July 16, 2018), https://www.uspto.gov/trademarks-getting-started/trademark-basics/trademarks-what-happens-next.

- TrafFix Devices, Inc. v. Mktg. Displays, Inc., 532 U.S. 23 (2001).

- Tuxedo Monopoly, Inc. v. General Mills Fun Group, Inc., 648 F.2d 1335 (C.C.P.A. 1981).

- Two Pesos, Inc. v. Taco Cabana, 505 U.S. 763 (1992).

- United Drug Co. v. Theodore Rectanus Co., 248 U.S. 90 (1918).

- U.S. PAT. AND TRADEMARK OFF., TRADEMARK MANUAL OF EXAMINING PROCEDURE (TMEP) § 1209.01 (2017).

- VIP Products, LLC v. Jack Daniel's Properties, Inc., 219 F.Supp.3d 891 (D. Ariz. 2018).

- Visa, U.S.A., Inc. v. Birmingham Trust Nat'l Bank, 696 F.2d 1371 (Fed. Cir. 1982).

- Wawa, Inc. v. Haaf, 40 U.S.P.Q.2d (BNA) 1629 (E.D. Pa. 1996).

- William Spieler, *Nominative Fair Use in Trademark Law: A Fair Use Like No Other* 89 J. PAT. & TRADEMARK OFF. SOC'Y 780 (2007).

- W. Scott Creasman, *Establishing Geographic Rights in Trademarks Based on Internet Use*, 95 TRADEMARK REP. 1016 (2005).

www.ingramcontent.com/pod-product-compliance
Lightning Source LLC
Chambersburg PA
CBHW030814180526
45163CB00003B/1279